DESTINED TO SURVIVE

A Memoir of Tragedies and Triumphs

Leslie Pobee

ISBN 979-8-88644-300-4 (Paperback)
ISBN 979-8-88644-301-1 (Digital)

Scripture references marked NKJV are from the
New King James Version. Copyright © 1982,
Thomas Nelson, Inc. Used by permission.

Covenant Books
11661 Hwy 707
Murrells Inlet, SC 29576
www.covenantbooks.com

DEDICATION

My life has been impacted by many great women, and I dedicate this book to them. First, to my biological mother, the late Dorothy Barbara Yaa Kwakyewa Ayeh. You were one of a kind—strong, hardworking, never giving up, loving, and very caring. I wish you were around to see me and Barbara complete college, get married, and have children. I can only imagine how happy you would have been if you had lived to see us achieve so much in life. But the lessons you taught me in the very short time you had with us, anchored, guided and urged me on all through my darkest moments. I fondly remember the many stories you told me in the evenings, the beautiful stories about your life as a young lady, your family, and your struggles. You were not ashamed to talk about your mistakes, failures, and successes, which became very useful as I grew up. Those lessons made it effortless for me to recognize the common mistakes of the youth and adopt measures to avoid them.

I remember how your siblings spoke so highly and fondly about you when they met me and Barbara after all those years. Although they were sad about your passing, they were happy to have had you in their lives in their youth. They told me about your readiness to go the extra mile for them whenever they needed your help. It made me so proud that you were my mother. I wrote this book to memorialize your name and love. Thank you, "Sister"—you have a very special place in our hearts.

Second, to Maa Nuva, our substitute mother in Liberia. You perfectly deputized our mother when we were lost and hopeless. As a mother, you protected us when news got out that we were Ghanaians and provided all our needs even with your limited resources. Sadly, I lost your contact when I got to Ghana, and I could not reach out to you. Barbara and I are forever grateful!

Third, to our adopted mother, Maa Doris. You just didn't take us into your home, but into your heart. You loved and cared for me and Barbara as if we were your flesh and blood. You stood firmly by us through all the tough times; supporting us financially when we needed it the most. I remember how you supported me when I was getting married and generously gave us a house to live in; not even to rent. We owe our life and successes to you, Mom. I love and cherish you so much. You are a rare gem, and I couldn't have asked for any other mother like you. Thank you very much!

Fourth, to our caretaker mother, Aunt Beatrice. We were so close that people at church thought you were my mother at a point. You took me to church and helped me find my feet in those early days of my stay at Mamprobi. You schooled me in the word of God, always bringing verses of scripture from your bible classes for us to read and discuss at home. Your fervency in prayer, praise, and patience in the face of adversity was extraordinary. I love you, Aunty B!

Fifth, to our late grandmother, Ms. Cecilia Obeng. You were the embodiment of our mother's love, going to great lengths to ensure that I was okay when I went to high school. Since I was away in a boarding school—it was never like home—you always provided all the extra items I needed to make my stay comfortable. You did all you could to help me forget about my pains and sorrow. You always wanted to have us over for the holidays. I love you, Grandma!

Sixth, to my dear wife, Ruth. I love you very much and thank you for standing by and with me through all these years.

Finally, to my one and only sister, Barbara. Thank you for being there with me on this journey. I don't know how life would have been without you. We were placed in the same family for a purpose, and I am glad we stayed connected. We've had our moments of sorrow and laughter all along this journey. I love you, my sister!

CONTENTS

Foreword..vii
Acknowledgment ix
Introduction..xi

Chapter 1: The Holiday Roosters...1
Chapter 2: Seeking Greener Pastures..11
Chapter 3: The First Civil War 22
Chapter 4: The Firestone Camp...28
Chapter 5: The Escape...33
Chapter 6: The Perilous Journey 41
Chapter 7: A Breath of Hope 51
Chapter 8: The Rescue...56
Chapter 9: The Journey 60
Chapter 10: Our New Home..64
Chapter 11: My Reflections 71

Bibliography...81

FOREWORD

To many people, the Liberian civil war was just another event in a sea of all-too-familiar reports of unrest on a continent plagued by numerous disasters. To us, it was a very real and harrowing experience we did not have the luxury of watching snippets of on our television sets in the *Evening News*.

It was a nightmare we lived in that did not end when we awoke at the break of dawn from an equally restless and troubled sleep. In its wake, lots of lives were lost, many people maimed, and everyone left mentally traumatized. It displaced citizens, tore families apart, and made orphans of many. We were among those to receive this new and unfortunate status.

What began for us as a loving mother's simple wish to keep her family safe and catered for during a manmade disaster, ended on a somber note of unimaginable tragedy. Now over thirty years later, Leslie offers, in this memoir, a vicarious experience of those frightening days and nights as he recounts the horrible experience. With the benefit of hindsight, he unpacks the events that led to us losing everything, which represented security and stability in our young lives, and discovers an underlying theme: the strong hand of a merciful God who kept showing up in ways and places we least expected Him to and herding us to safety, for no other reason than that He had predestined that these two newly orphaned children would not only survive a war in which even adults fully capable of fending for themselves lost their lives but would also be given a chance at succeeding in life.

Today, wars still beset us, and trouble is ever present among us. Take but a cursory look around and it is so easy to get discouraged. This is why I believe this memoir could not have been written at a more opportune time, or by a person better equipped through his experience of adversity to bear out the good that may be born of our afflictions. The reason is simple: he has himself experienced this and lived to testify of God's goodness.

If, during a bleak period in your life, you chance on *Destined to Survive: A Memoir of Tragedies and Triumphs*, may the reading of this book remind you that the God who watches over sparrows and numbers the very hair on our heads is always near us and takes a deep interest in everything dear to us. In seemingly bad times when all implementable options fail or perhaps *especially* then, He steps in when all hope is lost, raises new avenues of deliverance and salvation that we could never in our wildest dreams have fathomed, and causes our not-so-bright decisions to work for our good.

And like the people on whose hearts God placed the desire to help us when we needed urgent help, may He soften your heart to be a vessel of His loving-kindness, giving solace to whomever, He places in your path. God bless you!

Barbara Pobee
Accra, Ghana

ACKNOWLEDGMENT

Like any dream, the conception, gestation, and birth of a book is a wonderful process that takes the efforts of so many people. My deepest appreciation goes out to:

Keith and Lisa Walker for encouraging me to write my story, after sharing and reliving the horrors of my life with them. They also connected me to Laurel West, who helped me to shape my thoughts and ideas.

Kimi Grant for reading through my initial draft, helping me define my audience, and advising me on potential publishers.

My family and friends, unnamed and unnumbered but not forgotten, whose insights, wisdom, enthusiasm, and suggestions helped shape my life and thought process.

And most importantly, to you, for finding and reading this book.

INTRODUCTION

I battled with the idea of documenting the events that occurred in the first fifteen years of my life for many years. My main hesitation was due to the heart-wrenching memories the thought gave me; the memories were too painful for me to relive all by myself. Sharing my story with friends and at Christian gatherings was very easy because I learned to share it without letting my emotions have the best of me. However, I could just not muster the courage to sit all by myself to write a single sentence of this story. I was simply too afraid of my past; it traumatized me! Sharing my story to an audience was always therapeutic, and to me, that was sufficient. It was not until I shared the story with my pastor in 2017, and he asked me to share it at one of our prayer meetings, did I see the need to develop an outline. Writing that outline was a real struggle, but I managed to get it done.

After the prayer meeting, some friends encouraged me to put this story into a book so that many more people could benefit from my experience. Still afraid of the memories, I thought I should reach out to some writers in the church to find out if they were available to ghostwrite my book. Sadly, they were all fully booked for about a year. I felt I had already waited too long and didn't want to waste any more time. I decided to face my fears and just write this book. The process was very hard for me; I had to walk away from my computer on many occasions because I couldn't hold back my tears and I didn't want my wife or children to go find out why I was sobbing. Thankfully, after over thirty years, I finally completed this book, and I am extremely excited about it.

This story is about my family's experience during the first Liberian civil war that occurred in the early 1990s, which completely decimated our family and changed the trajectory of those of us who survived. It tore our family apart, subjected us to a prolonged period of hunger and starvation, led to the murder of our parents and brother, and destroyed our well-choreographed life and future. Although we only spent a year in that war, the effects of the war are still being experienced.

Physically, my sister and I became seriously malnourished and immunocompromised, and our bodies were ravaged by diseases. As the oldest of three children, I was greatly affected because I witnessed everything. It broke my sense of security and certainty and made me very fearful of the future. The war also stole my childhood and forced me into adulthood prematurely. This marked the beginning of decades of untold suffering and hardships. At that time, I wasn't prepared to start thinking and worrying about adults' stuff, like where my next meal was coming from and where I was going to stay.

By a miracle, my sister and I were saved from a near-death experience and were sheltered by a Liberian woman for a little over a month. We were later found and taken back to Ghana by the Ghana Armed Forces. Even after we returned to Ghana, my sense of insecurity and uncertainty didn't cease, it rather became worse. Sadly, the person who was assigned with the responsibility to take us home and reunite us with our family didn't gather all the information he needed before volunteering to bring us home. He left us with a stranger—someone we didn't know, who wasn't related to us, knew anything about us, or what we had been through up until that point. His reason was that he only had a few days in Ghana before returning to his duty post in Liberia and couldn't look for our relatives.

After staying in our new home for a little over a year, I was found by one of our uncles, which was also another miracle. However, the prevailing circumstances at the time made it unwise for me to leave and stay with our relatives, as that meant that I would have to leave my sister with our adopted parents—something I had vowed never to do, particularly because she was my only family and I did not want to lose her for anything. We stayed with our new parents until we both got married and left home.

Among the many reasons for writing this memoir, I want this story to encourage and assure you that there is hope for a brighter future if you will only remain steadfast in the face of insurmountable challenges. There is a Father who cares about your well-being and will come through for you if you will only let Him.

Be blessed!

CHAPTER 1

The Holiday Roosters

The year 1991 was ending; a year that I could only describe as full of uncertainties. My sister, Barbara, and I had been with our adopted parents for a little over a year, and things were beginning to look normal for me again. I could not shake off the lingering questions about what was happening to me and where my life was headed. Again, I wondered whether I could fulfill that childhood dream of becoming a great person and traveling the world. My life had completely changed, forcing me to wake up to my new normal life of adulthood, a trajectory that I was not prepared for. I had started going to church and taking interest in the messages I was hearing. I had also started searching the Scriptures with the hope of finding answers to the many questions I had.

The euphoria of the holiday season gave me a sense of hope that the new year, 1992, would bring me some answers. As the tradition was, my adopted mother purchased four roosters for our Christmas and New Year holiday meals that year; two were slaughtered for Christmas, and we were waiting for New Year's Eve to slaughter the other two. On Saturday mornings, as was my routine, I went to La, a suburb of Accra-Ghana, to clean up my adopted father's house, where they normally spent their weekends. The morning of Saturday, December 28, 1991, was not different. I woke up at my usual time, took a bath, and headed off to La. After the day's work at La, I returned to Mamprobi, the suburb of Accra we lived in, had my lunch, and went straight to the kitchen to help Aunty Naami (Beatrice), the caretaker, to complete the meal and help my adopted mother prepare for their weekend stay at La. She usually went with Barbara, who was two years old at the time, and Patience, a ten-year-old girl who stayed with her. As the oldest child in the house, I did most of the work in and around the house, so my Saturdays were very busy.

The late Mr. Nii Annan, my adopted mother's driver, who also lived at La, had arrived a few minutes earlier to pick them up. When we were done with the meals, I helped my adopted mother pack and cart the meals and the other things she was taking to La to the car. When they left, I decided to take a break under the big almond tree in the yard before going on to my next set of chores. As I sat down facing the direction of the chicken coop, I realized that the two roosters were still in the coop. They had not been taken out that day because I left earlier that morning for La, and when I returned, I did not remember to take them out. I quickly got up and went to attend to them. It was late in the afternoon, and I felt that they were starving. I put some water in their trough and placed it in the coop and stood by for them to drink. When they were done, I put some grains of corn in their feeding trough and was about to put it in the coop, when I thought to myself, *Let me just bring them out to feed and roam about in the yard, while I kept an eye on them.*

The yard was walled and large enough to give them plenty of room to roam about, pick up inserts, and pluck some leaves from the low plants. I found a rope in the house and tied their feet, one to the other. I assumed that they were not that intelligent to coordinate their movement to get out of the yard. Moreover, the wall was pretty high, and I did not believe that the roosters could fly over it and escape. Even if they attempted to, they would get trapped by a plant or something in the yard and would not wander far off. Boy, was I wrong!

As I watched them for a while, my mind drifted off into one of my many contemplations. After a few minutes, I realized that the roosters were nowhere in sight. I got up and started looking for them. I looked in all the open spaces in the yard, but I could not find them.

We had a big garden in the house and thought they might have gone in there. But my search in the garden also did not yield any results. I became alarmed, and my cursory search for the roosters turned frantic. I started to search every little inch of the yard. I needed to find those roosters as soon as possible because they could be stolen or run over by a car as our house was near a very busy street. If that were to happen, I was going to get my due—something I wanted to avoid at all costs.

I searched everywhere in the yard for about fifteen minutes, but I could not find those roosters. Those fifteen minutes felt like forever! I became increasingly anxious with every passing minute, but instead of thinking about finding the roosters, I began to think about the consequences of not finding them. I started to think of possible explanations I would give for letting the roosters loose because the way I tied them that day was not right. I usually tied them to an immovable object when they were out of their coop.

Where could these roosters be? I thought to myself. *These walls are pretty high and there was no way those roosters could have flown over it together. I don't think anyone had also entered the yard because the gate to the yard made a lot of squeaking noises when opening and my attention would have been drawn to the gate if someone had entered the yard.*

As I thought about where the roosters could be, I remembered that there was a hole in the northeastern corner of the wall. I had sealed it off with some thatch branches I cut from a palm tree and secured it with a few stones. The hole was very small; not something I believed those two big roosters could go through, especially when their legs were tied together, but I went to check there anyway. When I got there, the roosters were not there, and there was no sign that the thatch had been disturbed. That broken portion of the wall was close to the entrance of one of our neighbor's yards, so I thought that I should go to that house to find out whether anyone had seen the roosters.

The houses on our side of the block had a south-facing entrance and our neighbor's house was north-facing, meaning I had to go southward through our gate and turn toward the north to get to our neighbor's house. Fortunately, there was another entrance to our neighbor's house; it was smaller, and it had no gate. I felt that a lot could happen on my blindside as I went all the way, but at that point, that was the only option I had. When I got to the broken part of the wall from the outside, there the roosters were. I was surprised! It felt as if someone had picked them up and placed them on the other side of the wall just at the time I got there so I could find them. There was no way those roosters could have gone through that hole; it was impossible! I was baffled! Up to this day, I still cannot make sense of how those roosters got on the other side of the wall.

As soon as the roosters saw me approaching, they ran into our neighbor's yard, and I followed them. Just when I got onto our neighbor's yard, I met one of my uncles—McAdams Ntim. I had not seen him for more than three years, but we recognized each other as soon as we locked eyes. He was just done having a haircut and got out of the barber's chair to leave when I appeared in the yard. As soon as McAdams saw me, he exclaimed in Twi, "Kofi! What are you doing here and where is Sister?"

Kofi was the name my mother's family called me because I was born on a Friday, and "Sister," was what my biological mother's family called her. I just stood there in shock and bewilderment as I stared at him, shaking my head. When he saw me shaking my head, he knew exactly what that meant. A rim of moisture crept over his eyes, and he quickly wiped off his tears. At that point, we both stood there silently for a moment, then the barber interrupted the silence by asking McAdams whether he knew me. He responded in the affirmative and added that I am his nephew; the son of his elder sister who took him to Liberia.

With mixed emotions, McAdams introduced me to the barber, whom I already knew as Eben-T, as a very good friend he knew from Monrovia, Liberia. He was one of the Ghanaian returnees from Liberia. He lost all his belongings during the first Liberian civil war, which occurred between 1989 to 1996 but was fortunate to return to Ghana safely with his family. He could not immediately get any employment, so to cater to his family, he went to our neighbor, to whom I believed he was related, and asked for a space to start a barbering salon. His wife, who was a Liberian, could not cope with the living conditions in Ghana and decided to return to Monrovia, leaving their three children with him.

Eben-T worked as a professional barber in Liberia, and not long after he returned, he began to get customers, most of whom were the friends he grew up with in Mamprobi. McAdams told me that he had been going to that salon every fortnight for the past eighteen months but had never seen me or heard about Barbara and me. The children in that house were my friends. I even attended the same junior high school with a boy—Benjamin, who was known as Junior—in the house, so I used to go there often, but not once did our paths cross. According to McAdams, he always used the north entrance to the yard and had never used the south entrance to the barbering salon. He added that he was really in a hurry that day, and he decided to park on the street near the south entrance to the salon. The south entrance was the entrance I also used to get to the house because it was closer to my house. I used the north entrance only when Junior and I were returning from school.

All this while the roosters had gotten entangled by a twig in our neighbor's yard and could no longer move. I kept an eye on them as we talked with Eben-T. When we were done talking to Eben-T, McAdams asked where I lived so he could introduce himself to my guardians. I told him my adopted parents had gone to La for the weekend, but the caretaker, Aunty Beatrice (B), was at home. I picked up the roosters, and we turned and walked to the house. I opened the gate and ushered him into the yard and walked to the back of the house, where Aunty B was and introduced him to her as my uncle. They exchanged a few pleasantries and through the conversation, we even realized that Aunty B's late husband was married to a nephew of my grandpa. It felt like a family reunion that day. After a few minutes of interaction, McAdams sought her permission to bring me to his house at Korle Gonno, another suburb of Accra, to spend a few hours with his family. It was only about 2.4 kilometers (1.5 miles) away. Aunty B was familiar with that neighborhood and even knew some people at the house McAdams lived at. She readily agreed to let McAdams bring me to his house for a few hours. He promised to bring me back home later that evening.

After driving for about ten minutes, we arrived at Korle Gonno, the neighborhood McAdams lived in. As a returnee himself, he lost all his belongings during the war but was fortunate to return safely to Ghana with his family. He did not have any house in Ghana, hence, he had to live temporarily at Korle Gonno with his in-laws. His family of five was crammed in a single bedroom with a small living area, sharing a common outer restroom with the other families living in the house.

I was completely speechless when I saw McAdams' living conditions. It was a stark difference from how he lived in Monrovia. He had been completely reduced to nothing! He lived like a king in Liberia in a two-story rented house, with two large living areas on both floors in a middle-class neighborhood of Monrovia. As a professional hairstylist, his salon, which was located on the ground floor was fully air-conditioned. He dressed like a bank executive every day to work. His wife, who was a stay-home mom, occasionally joined him in the saloon whenever she was bored staying upstairs all by herself with the children. When she was in the saloon, she assisted him with the cashier duty.

After spending about two hours with his family, we agreed that McAdams will pick me up after church service the following day, which was a Sunday, to go to meet my adopted parents. He dropped me off at Mamprobi, and he told Aunty B about our plans for Sunday, to which she agreed. That evening, as I lay on my mat to sleep, I could not get the day's events out of my mind. I was happy that I was finally going to meet my relatives after about ten years; however, I felt very uneasy about the whole idea of McAdams and me going to meet my adopted parents. I was worried about how my adopted parents were going to receive the news that I have met my uncle, as well as how my relatives would react when they saw me.

I wondered what my relatives' living conditions would be like; particularly after I saw McAdams living conditions. I wondered whether I was prepared to move in with them. On the other hand, I did not feel at home with my adopted parents at that time. I had no relationship with them, even after staying with them for a little over a year. I could not freely talk to them about anything, not even my concerns. They also did not find out what I was going through; I felt abandoned. I felt that the relationship I had with my adopted parents was a master-servant relationship where I was given a set of instructions and chores to do in the morning when they were going to work, and I was expected to complete them by the time they return in the evening. There was also that feeling that I had to work for everything I got, even food. So I was caught in a dilemma!

Again, I knew very little about my adopted parents at that time. What I knew about them were stories I heard from other people rather than from themselves, including their standing in society and the jobs they did. I was at that stage where I needed a father figure in my life, someone to guide and help me navigate the turbulent adolescence period, but I did not get that from my adopted father. I also did not know anybody in the neighborhood, hence, I had to figure everything out by myself. I was also now learning to speak Ga, my native language, which meant that I could not freely communicate with people in our neighborhood. It made life very challenging for me.

These challenges caused me to miss my parents so much. Sometimes, I would just cry my heart out when I felt frustrated. I thought about all the great moments I had with my family before they were taken away from me. I longed to relive those moments. Apart from that, I used to daydream about living with my relatives— how I would have people to talk to, how I wouldn't have to work so hard every day; how I would have had plenty to eat and didn't have to beg for everything I needed. I was sure that my relatives did not know that Barbara and I were alive and living in Accra; they would have reached out to us if they knew. I used to imagine asking my grandma where all my cousins, aunties, and uncles were.

I also remembered the times I spoke to my friends at school about my story and how I wish I could reach out to my relatives. On one of those occasions, Emmanuel, a friend at school told me he had family living in Nungua, the suburb my relatives lived in, and he visited them once a while. Emmanuel made me understand it was pretty far, about twenty-four kilometers away, and I needed to have enough money to board another bus at the main terminal at Accra.

I did not have money, so he promised that he will try to look for my family whenever he visited his family at Nungua since they lived pretty closed to where my relatives lived. I gave him directions to the house and a description of the house. I also gave him the names of some of my relatives, including my grandma, with the hope that when he found them, he will let them know we were alive and living at Mamprobi.

Sometime later, Emmanuel visited Nungua and according to him, he followed my directions, went to the neighborhood, and found the house, but he did not meet anyone at home that day. I was glad that at least he found the house, which meant that whenever I had the means and the opportunity, I could find the house. I desperately wanted to figure out how I could reach out to my relatives, therefore, meeting McAdams that day was a dream come through. As all these thoughts went through my mind, I fell asleep.

After church service that Sunday, McAdams picked me up, and we went to La to meet my adopted parents. My adopted mother was not at home that afternoon. She had gone for her high school old girls meeting with Barbara. I told my adopted dad what happened the previous day and how I met my uncle. He wasn't that excited about the news because it was telling on his face, however, he maintained his composure throughout the period. My adopted father told McAdams his side of the story—how we went to live with him, how he had searched for our relatives by putting our story and our description in the local newspapers, but no one had come forward to claim us as their relatives. Since he wanted us to continue our education, he decided to let us stay in his house because he could not give us to just anyone.

My adopted father stated, "I knew that this day would come when Sowah [my middle name] would find his relatives. To avoid any future legal battles and make their return to you easy, I did not formalize their adoption. If Sowah wants, he can go stay with you, that's fine, but I would like to keep Barbara because she has bonded very well with my wife."

Just then, McAdams turned to me as in getting an answer, but I shook my head in disapproval. I added that "Barbara is the only family I had and I wouldn't want to be separated from her" for any reason, particularly because of all we have been through together. I had also told myself sometime earlier that Barbara was never going to leave my side until we were old enough to go our separate ways. I realized that if I agree, I might lose that sibling bond I had with her forever. At that time, I was already sensing efforts to drive a wedge between Barbara and me; a situation that would have gotten worse if I had agreed to leave her with them. When they realized that I would not oblige, they changed the topic. McAdams then sought my adopted father's permission to bring me to see my family at Nungua. My adopted father agreed and got up from his seat to see us off to the door. As we left, I noticed the look of displeasure on my adopted father's face.

We traveled for about thirty minutes and arrived at my grandparents' neighborhood around 1:30 p.m. It was different from the neighborhood I knew as a child. The community was completely built up, and most of the vegetation I thought was there had been cleared. I thought to myself, *It would have been very difficult for me to find my way here if I had attempted to go here all by myself.* I also began to doubt Emmanuel's claim that he visited the house but met no one at home because many people were living in the house.

There were no telephones or mobile phones in those days, so McAdams did not tell his mother (Cecilia) that he had found us. When we arrived, she was at the back of the house doing some gardening. I remember us going through the kitchen to the back of the house where grandma was. After greeting her, he asked her whether she knew me. She responded in the negative. McAdams asked her to take a good look at me. She stared at me, but she did not recognize me. Then he told her, "This is Kofi, Sister's oldest son."

She said, "Stop those silly jokes of yours!"

"Seriously, this is Kofi!"

Then she looked at me again and jumped up to hug me. I cannot describe how excited my grandmother was that day. It was like she had won a lottery! She was very happy to see me and to know that at least two members of her oldest daughter's family were still alive. I saw her becoming emotional.

"I was always praying and pleading with God to give me, at least, one person from Sister's family, but through his bountiful mercy He gave me two," she said. "I could not bring myself to terms with the fact that all five members of your family had perished," she added.

"Thank you, God. I now know You heard my prayers," She concluded.

My grandmother told me she had wept so much about us that her tear ducts were no longer producing tears. She also became hypertensive in the process. She wanted to know all about how Barbara and I went back to Ghana, how we ended up in a stranger's house rather than her house.

She said it was time to prepare dinner, so we should go to the kitchen. As we walked to the kitchen, McAdams said he will leave because he had to meet a friend in another suburb of Accra.

In the remaining chapters, I will tell you about how it all began—how my parents immigrated to Liberia; the tragedy that befell them, how Barbara and I became orphans, and how we found our way into the house of a couple who were not our relatives.

CHAPTER 2

Seeking Greener Pastures

In the 1970s and early 1980s, Ghana went through a period of political, economic, and environmental crises. The country experienced several coup d'états and to make matters worse, this was followed by a prolonged period of drought and famine. The once-thriving state that Ghana was had quickly sunk to the bottom to a point where it was on the trajectory of becoming a failed state. Many Ghanaians were compelled to travel abroad, to any place under the sun that was not called Ghana, to seek greener pastures. During that period, the economy of Nigeria had improved tremendously because of the increased world oil prices, which brought in a steady flow of revenue, making the country Africa's wealthiest nation. The improvement in the economy was accompanied by an increase in the standard of living, attracting Nigerians living in rural areas, as well as foreign nationals from the West African sub-region, especially, Ghanaians. Nigeria was very attractive to teachers, and my parents, both of whom were trained teachers, took advantage of the opportunity to seek greener pastures. My mother, Dorothy Barbara Ayeh, affectionately known as Sister by her family, also attempted to make the trip to Nigeria to seek greener pastures.

According to my mother, traveling to Nigeria legally at the time was very expensive; she needed to secure a job in Nigeria before she could apply for a visa. Again, she needed to have enough money in her account to prove that she could support herself in Nigeria for at least two months before she received her first pay. However, using one of the many illegal routes was less costly but pretty dangerous. Besides, unlike these days where we have access to the internet and can easily apply for overseas jobs, in those days, they had to write letters, travel, sometimes for miles, just to post letters. They also had to wait for months to receive replies.

Mother opted for the illegal option as that was cheaper, and she could get into Nigeria and find a job. She was introduced to a middleman, with whom she planned, paid for, and set a date for her journey. She was in the company of other young Ghanaians traveling to Nigeria to seek greener pastures. They traveled on the road leading to Aflao, in the Volta Region of Ghana to Lomé in Togo, and then onward through the Seme border between the Republic of Benin and Nigeria.

When they arrived at the Seme border, the driver stopped and told them that that was how far he could go. They all got off the vehicle they were traveling on, and they had to enter Nigeria on foot through the unapproved routes. They could not go as a group but had to be given to individual smugglers on the Benin side of the border, who knew the unapproved routes into Nigeria. She paid the young man who was to help her get into Nigeria, and they entered the bush in the dark. After walking for a while, the smuggler tried to rape Mom. He knocked her down to the ground, put a bunch of sand into her mouth, and he tore her clothes in an attempt to rape her. Luckily for Mom, she was wearing a pair of gens pants (trousers), which she had fastened with a belt that was buckled at her back. In the struggle, she used her knees to hit his scrotum, got him off her, and ran into the dark.

Mother didn't have a map of the country nor did she know exactly where she was going in Nigeria. Nobody was also meeting her on the Nigerian side of the border. Fearing for her life, she decided to return to the border crossing instead of going any further into Nigeria. Using her knowledge of geography, she was able to find her way back to the border crossing into Benin, where she was handed over to the smuggler. Fortunately for her, the vehicle she traveled in was still parked at the motel they were dropped off. She found the driver and explained her ordeal to him. Our mother's clothes were torn and she had bruises on a body. Luckily, she found a clothes shop and she got herself a shirt to buy.

The driver agreed to bring her back to Accra free of charge since she did not achieve her goal. This was how her dream of seeking greener pastures in Nigeria ended. But Mom, the determined mother I knew, did not give up; she kept looking for other opportunities to travel again.

Traveling to Liberia

Sometime later, my mother met a friend who told her about job prospects in Liberia. Around that time, my dad had also gone to Nigeria, but nobody knew exactly where he was. As I mentioned earlier, the postal system was the only means of communicating with the outside world, so when someone was living outside and did not have a postal address, they could not easily communicate with their relatives and loved ones back home. Not long after our mother was unable to get into Nigeria, the country began to face its economic crisis. They began to blame African migrants, especially Ghanaians, for the failing economy. Politicians began to spread the falsehood that Ghanaians had taken all the jobs and brought crime to Nigeria. This led to a serious xenophobic uprising and attacks on foreign nationals in Nigeria, particularly Ghanaians. And that was when the notorious expression "Ghana must go" gained momentum in Nigeria.

During that period, the crises in Ghana had worsened, and the country was close to becoming a failed state. People were forced to leave the country to anywhere other than Ghana. Nothing was working. There was no money, and even if people had money, it was worth nothing because there was no food to buy—grocery stores were empty and people had to queue for hours for almost everything. Mother decided to give the thought of traveling out of Ghana a try again because life in Ghana was tough.

Somewhere between 1979 and 1980, my mother had saved enough money to enable her to travel again; this time, to Liberia, which is located to the west of Ghana. She traveled through the Ivory

Coast into Liberia but legally this time. I remember Mother recounting some of the ordeals she suffered at the hands of the immigration officials at the border crossing between Ghana, the Ivory Coast, and Liberia. They extorted money and manhandled people. They had to go through a series of checks to safely enter Liberia. Fortunately, this time, she had some help from friends; they helped her to secure a teaching job, and soon, she was earning enough and could send some money and food items to her parents and siblings. I was staying with Cecilia, my grandma, at the time. That was to ensure that I was well fed and catered to.

After about a year, my mother returned to Ghana and decided to bring McAdams, her younger brother, who had completed high school but could not continue his education because of financial challenges. Cecilia, my grandma, had already retired and could not afford his tuition. Mom did not want him to stay at home and be influenced by bad company. She also felt that she could help McAdams learn a trade in Liberia. My mother went with me this time because she had McAdams babysit me when she had to go out. Luckily, she found McAdams an apprenticeship position as a hairstylist.

I stayed with Mom for a while in Bomi Hills, now Bomi County, until McAdams completed his apprenticeship and had to move to Monrovia. Around that time, my dad had also been forced to return home because of the xenophobic uprising and attacks in Nigeria and the resultant deportation of all Ghanaians. He had stayed home for a while and was not finding a job. Mom decided to bring me back to Ghana, leave me with my grandmother, Cecilia, and bring my dad to Liberia.

After staying for a while, my dad did not get a job, so Mom arranged with the Department of Education in Bomi Hills to swap job places with my dad. She was pregnant with my brother, and hence, used that as her maternity leave. Not soon after that, Mom returned to Ghana to give birth to my brother in June of 1982. After that, she returned to Liberia and started a grocery shop in Bomi Hills while my dad worked as a high school teacher in her place.

My parents moved to a bigger house and used the front area as a local shop. My mother was very skillful; she could sew both men's and women's articles of clothing and bake cakes, cookies, pies, and different pastries. She was also very entrepreneurial, and in no time, the local shop also flourished. However, because of thievery, she ran into losses. Sometime later, Mom decided to bring me back to Liberia to help her because I will be an extra eye on the business. That was also because my dad was almost always out of the house. Apart from his teaching job, he was also a registered soccer referee. As such, he was always officiating one match or another in and around Bomi Hills.

Sometime toward the end of 1982, Mom flew home to Ghana to celebrate my seventh birthday, which was in about two weeks. I remember that she was to arrive in Accra on a Friday, and the economic crisis in the country was at its peak. Because of the many mouths (my cousins and sometimes their parents) my grandmother had to feed, we ate once a day; usually around late afternoon. In the morning, we drank some porridge or "ntensinu," the stock that was left after boiling "kenkey," a local Ghanaian meal made from fermented corn dough. We hardly got sugar to put in the breakfast, let alone milk. We had those things when Mom shipped us supplies as she was the only member of the family who was gainfully employed at that time. Both grandparents had retired at that time. My aunties contributed to our meals when they went out and found a day's labor to get some money.

At dawn that Friday, there was a severe rainstorm and one of the main electric cables providing electricity to our neighborhood broke and we lost power. When Grandpa woke up that morning, he drove to the sub office of the Ghana Electricity Corporation, as it was known in those days, to report the problem. He did not meet the officers-in-charge at the sub office, so he continued to the head office at Accra. That took almost the entire day.

At about 1:30 p.m., Grandma started preparing the day's meal. We were to have fufu, a local dish prepared from boiled and pounded cassava and plantains, with soup (chicken soup). After Grandma peeled the cassava and the plantains, as the oldest grandchild among my cousins (about six years old), I was responsible for disposing of the peels. We had a neighbor who reared goats and sheep, so Grandma asked me to carry the peels to our neighbor to feed the animals. When I picked the basket of peels to set off, one of my cousins, Kwame, who was about five years old, started following me. With my childish mind, I tried to talk him out of the idea of following me. The reason was that when I went alone, I had the lion's share of whatever treats that were given, but if I went with some of my cousins, I had to share the treats with them equally. Knowing this, Kwame was determined to follow me. I tried all the "tricks in the book" to get him to return but he would not.

The neighborhood was sparsely populated, and the houses were far apart. There were a lot of bushes in between the houses, but the neighborhood was very safe. Grandpa, Seth K. Botchway, was a police commissioner in the Ghana Police Force, so no criminal dared to commit any crime in our neighborhood. We walked for about two to three minutes and had gone past the second house from our house when we got to a bushy area. When I looked up, I saw a cable hanging from a pole somewhere in the bushes. I decided to try another trick on Kwame to get him to return. I told him the broken cable I saw was a snake that could attack him if he does not return.

The cable hanged loosely from the pole, and out of ignorance, I told Kwame I could touch the snake but it will not harm me. Even if it attacked us, I could run faster and leave him behind. With that, we got off the trail and walked toward the hanging cable. I turned toward the cable with the hope that Kwame would return, but he followed me into the bush. When we got closer to the cable, I bent over, holding the basket on my head, and with my right hand, I picked up the cable. I don't know what happened to me, all I remember was that I was laying on my back, under the cable facing the sky. The cable was across my chest, and I was being jolted.

Sadly, the ground was also wet because of the rain that fell that dawn, which made matters even worse; the entire area was electrically charged. It felt like my body was experiencing a sudden tremor or vibration; I could not control myself. It felt like I was burning, and there was an inexplicable general tightening around my body—I was dying! I don't know how long I laid under that cable, but it felt like forever. Kwame stood there watching helplessly but he did not try to touch me. I saw him standing there as I lay on the floor. I felt that I was screaming and calling out for help but not even Kwame heard my voice. Thankfully, he did not attempt to touch me. If he had attempted to, he may have been killed because he was barefooted.

Where I lay was a bit far from the nearest path, and as I said earlier, there weren't a lot of people living in our neighborhood at that time. Again, due to the economic hardship, people seldom walked around in the neighborhood. This made my chances of being found very slim. Not long after that, a man appeared in my side view as I lay on the ground, then he turned and went away. I was very disappointed because I thought he had come to help me. Not long after that, Kwame also took off and ran away. At that point, I felt abandoned, but just then I saw the man in my side view again, this time holding a cassava stem. When Kwame saw the man returning with the main stem of a cassava plant, he thought the man was going to spank him, so he ran. The man uprooted the stem from a nearby cassava garden when he went away and broke off the leaves and roots. It was just about the time I felt that I was losing my breath. He stood at a distance, and with the cassava stem, lifted the electric cable from across my chest and hands and threw it a distance away from where I lay.

He bent over and lifted me to my feet, but I fainted. At that point, the man picked me up and placed me on his shoulders, and ran onto the footpath that led back to my grandparents' house. I think he might have taken notice of the direction Kwame ran in. Sometime later, I gained consciousness and noticed that I was in the man's arms and that we were headed toward our house. I became very dark, and I had severe burns on the palms of my hands, around my thumb and index fingers, and across my chest. I still have some of the scars, especially on my left thumb and index fingers. The man rushed me to the nearest house, and they directed him to my grandparents' house.

Meanwhile, I suspected that when Kwame got home, he did not tell Grandma about what had happened. He just went and joined my cousins and our friends who were playing outside the kitchen and told them, "Ehh heh! Kofi said I should not follow him to Aunty Aggies's house. A man with a big stick is beating him."

Grandma overheard their conversation but thought it was just child's play and did not pay any attention to him. Within a few minutes, Grandma said she heard the voice of a young man calling out loudly, "Whose son is this? I found him laying under the electric cable that broke and was laying on the ground in the bush."

When Grandma heard the noise, out of curiosity, she went out to see what was happening. When she got to the front of the house, she saw me in the man's arms. Grandma panicked and quickly ran to the young man, took me out of his arms, and set me on a chair that was on the front porch of our house. Grandma was just screaming, "Lord, have mercy, Lord, have mercy!"

I was so weak, but conscious. The commotion drew the attention of some neighbors to our courtyard. Grandma was very scared and confused because Grandpa had been gone for the entire day, and worst of all, my mother was arriving later that evening. The thought of my mother arriving that night frightened her even more because she wondered about the explanation she would give her had the worst happened to me. As I stated above, the main purpose for which Mom was returning to Ghana was to celebrate my seventh birthday, which was in about two weeks, and my demise would have been very devastating, to say the least. She frantically called one of the boys at the house to run to the main road that led to our neighborhood to bring a taxi, and to another, she asked him to bring me some water to drink.

In my stupor, I overheard the man who brought me home telling someone that he was returning home from work—the Electricity corporation of Ghana (ECG)—when he saw me laying under the cable and went to my rescue. He even described his house to the person. But at that time, according to what I knew from those who went to work every day, the working hours were from 8:00 a.m. to 5:00 p.m., and no one got out of work at 2:00 p.m.—unless, of course, they went for an early morning shift, which was unlikely at the ECG. Moreover, Grandpa went to that sub office of the ECG that morning, but there was no one on site to attend to him and had to go to Accra. Besides, where I lay was nowhere close to the path the man was supposedly walking on, so he could not have found me. Again, the man said he lived in our neighborhood but no one there knew him.

The young man who was sent to get the taxi took so long that Grandma became very anxious. Fortunately, Grandpa arrived just when Grandma was losing it. Grandpa quickly whisked me into his Mercedes Benz, and together with Grandma, they drove me to the Korle Bu Teaching Hospital (KBTH). KBTH was very far from Nungua, but that was the best place I could be given the urgent care I needed. I don't remember what happened during the journey to KBTH, but I remembered that I was examined, my wounds were treated, given some medication, and scheduled to return the following Tuesday for a follow-up check-up. When my mother returned that evening, she was not excited by what happened that day but was glad that I was at least okay.

The following day, Mom and Grandma went in search of the man who brought me home. They followed the direction and the description of the house the man gave, but they did not find any house with that description and neither did they find him. Again, no one in that entire area worked at ECG. Who was that person and where was he? Those are questions that have not been answered to this day!

Instead of staying for two weeks, Mom decided that it was time to have me live with her in Liberia. Although she was thinking about it, the situation she found me in convinced her that it was time for me to live with her. Moreover, Grandma's workload had increased because at that point, she was already babysitting five grandchildren, and Mom felt I would not get the care I needed. Luckily, she had enough money on her, and she was able to change her return flight to enable me to get a seat on her return flight. We left for Monrovia the following weekend after I attended my Tuesday appointment. I remembered the doctor who examined me said that I needed to be admitted for a least two weeks and given some intravenous fluids because I was very dehydrated, but Mom said she was taking me to

Monrovia and have the doctors admit me on arrival. We said our goodbyes that weekend and left for Monrovia, Liberia.

I don't remember what happened during the trip, nor do I remember when we got to Liberia but all I remembered was that I woke up in the hospital in intensive care with a lot of intravenous fluids on me. My mother was sitting on my bed, and the first question I heard from her when I came around was "Why did you do this to me? You've made me very worried."

According to Mom, I had been in a coma for a while, I think for about a week or so, because I came around either on my birthday or a day after. When I opened my eyes, I saw my birthday balloons and presents around my bed. The nurses joined my mother to sing happy birthday to me. I was discharged a day or two after I came around. I remember my mother telling me that we even had a lay-over in Abidjan, Ivory Coast, and she had hoped that I would wake up to see the beautiful city, but I did not even open my eyes once.

After that incident, I don't remember anything that happened in the immediate months and years afterward, but I remembered that Mom had a flourishing grocery business, and I used to help her in the shop and carting supplies from some Lebanese stores located downtown Tubmanburg, the capital city of Bomi Hills (presently known as Bomi County), located northwest of Monrovia because we lived in one of the suburbs. The main road that went through the suburb led to the iron ore mines in Bomi Hills. I used to help her to sell her goods. Sometimes, I and another boy went hawking in and around the neighborhood, especially when the shop just started and people did not know about it. After people got to know about the shop and started going there to shop, I stopped hawking. My mother baked many different pastries and sewed both men's and women's items of clothing.

After a while, we started losing business; people were no longer patronizing the shop. Mom also became pregnant with my sister, Barbara, and she could no longer bake, sew, and do other things in the shop. I also became busy with school work and could not spend a lot of time in the shop. The people she hired to man the shop were also stealing the items, so Mom closed down the shop. Around that time, there were rumors that our dad was cheating on Mom with some of his students. Whenever she confronted him with the allegations, he denied them. She began to see proof from the pockets of his clothes, but he kept on denying it.

After she gave birth, we moved to another neighborhood in Tubmanburg. But our dad was still cheating on her and they were always quarreling. My mother decided to look for a teaching job in Monrovia and that will be her way of getting away from our dad for him to begin to reason again.

Not long after that, Mother found a job as the principal of an elementary school known as Golden Age International School in Gardnersville Estate, a suburb of Monrovia. She moved to Monrovia with my brother Kwabena (Peter) and my sister Barbara, but I stayed with my dad because she wanted me to complete the school year before joining her. This was a very significant development in my family because things were never the same after that. Our dad became sober and started going home early. He began to take interest in my school work and the other household chores that he had left Mom to do all by herself. I was eager to join Mom, so as soon as the school year ended, I traveled to Monrovia. I started ninth grade in Monrovia, and I was very excited about it because I got to live in the city. Our mother's salary was good enough to take care of all of us, and our lives improved dramatically. Meanwhile, our dad kept his job at Bomi Hills but visited us every fortnight. Since Bomi Hills was only about two and a half hours away from Monrovia, Dad began to visit us every Friday after a few months.

CHAPTER 3

The First Civil War

Barely two years into my mother's new job, the Liberian civil unrest started. It was initially thought to be a simple uprising that the Armed Forces of Liberia (AFL) could easily quash. Through propaganda, the Liberian government under the leadership of President Samuel Doe downplayed the uprising and assured the nation that the situation was under control. There was, however, more to the story than we were made to understand. There were initial reports that the government had quashed the uprising. On Sunday, December 24, 1989, Christmas Eve, we heard a public announcement that Charles Taylor's National Patriotic Front of Liberia (NPFL) had reentered Liberia from Guinea through Nimba County, which is north of Monrovia after they were initially chased out of the country.

People who could project the trend of events started to leave the country, but we could not. Returning to Ghana was virtually impossible because we had become a family of five and it would have cost a fortune to go back to Ghana. I am not sure our parents had saved up, either. Even if they had that much money, they could not access it because the banks were not operating. We could also not get a loan because there was very little economic activity at that time for anyone to have that amount of money to lend to my parents. Worst of all, we lived quite a distance from central Monrovia to be close to the Freeport and Roberts International Airport to have access to the outside world. The only thing Mom could do was to assure us that things were going to get better and that life would return to normalcy.

The government of Liberia, on the other hand, assured us that things were under control, but life gradually came to a standstill. Economic activities were interrupted, schools were closed, grocery shops could not restock, people stopped going to work, the power supply was interrupted, and then the water supply was also terminated. Our economic situation became dire. Within a few months, the uprising degenerated into a full tribal war between the Krahn tribe on one hand, and the Gio and Mano ethnic groups. The war progressively reached the outskirts of Monrovia, and our living conditions worsened. We were confined to our homes; children could not play with their friends and stepping out of the house to even enjoy the sunlight was risky. When we woke up in the morning, we had nothing to do, nothing to look forward to, and nowhere to go. It was such a hopeless situation. It felt like the country was sitting on a time bomb just waiting to explode.

Fortunately, Mom had purchased a 250-kilogram bag of rice sometime earlier, which she rationed to last a little longer than the time it normally would. When the bag of rice started to run out, she reduced our meals to a single meal instead of our regular three square meals a day. We could not keep a garden because we lived in a built-up suburb of Monrovia. We could not buy food; the shops were closed, and the farmers' markets were not operating. Even when some food was available, it was very expensive. In short, daily life and economic activities came to a complete halt, and we just braced ourselves for the worst.

At a point, we could not get updates from the radio stations in Liberia because most of them had closed down. The only news we could listen to was that of the Liberian Broadcasting System, popularly known as ELBC, which was spreading propaganda. To get reliable news, we all relied on international news media, such as the BBC's (British Broadcasting Corporation) *Focus on Africa* programming for updates. I remember that the community used to gather around a small battery-powered radio set. The owner of the radio set would place their alkaline batteries in the sun to recharge before using them. During the broadcast, we had updates of where the conflicts had reached and reports of all the atrocities committed on both sides of the conflict each day.

Somewhere in April 1990, the war reached the outskirts of Monrovia, which further reduced the already limited movement and travels we could do; we just remained sheltered in place. Our dad managed to travel to New Matadi Estate, where we lived, and spent that weekend with us. I think it was either the first or second weekend of June because we had not seen him for about a month. Upon realizing the seriousness of the situation in Monrovia and hearing rumors that the NPFL was closing in on Monrovia, he decided that he would return to Bomi Hills, put our remaining belongings there in order, and grab a few personal belongings, and return to Monrovia before the Friday of that week. Sadly, that was the last time we ever saw our dad or heard from him. Later on in 1991, when I met my uncle McAdams, he told me that a friend of his who lived in Monrovia but used to travel to Bomi Hills due to his business activities told him that when the NPFL reached Bomi Hills, someone gave our dad away as a Malian, and some rebel soldiers pounced on him, beat him with the butt of their rifles, and left him by a road in Bomi Hills to die. Our dad was tall and very dark in complexion, which was the common feature of the Malians who traded in that part of Liberia. The Malians were not liked at all by the locals because they were regarded as tricksters and fraudsters. The news was hard to bear because it brought back to mind the ordeal my family suffered. If our dad was with us, things may have turned out differently; maybe we could have all made it out alive. This just confirmed the kind of brutality the NPFL militias meted out on innocent civilians and foreigners during the Liberian civil.

As day broke that Monday morning, initially, everything seemed normal. We did not have running water, so we went out to brush our teeth with some of the rainwater we had collected in barrels outside our house and went back indoors. After a while, the atmosphere in the neighborhood became tense; as if something was about to happen. The men who normally patrolled our neighborhood were nowhere in sight that morning; there was some kind of uneasiness in the air. From the window of our house, we could see people whispering to the women who sold foodstuffs and other items on tabletops and they were rushing to take their wares down. We had not spoken to anybody that morning, so we just observed the strange movements from our window. It was like everything came to a stand-still all of a sudden, and people who tried to leave the neighborhood were turned back. Unknowingly, the NPFL rebels had surrounded our suburb and were just waiting for a signal to enter our neighborhood. Within a matter of minutes, the morning calm turned into sporadic gunshots and loud noises, and our quiet neighborhood was enveloped by total anarchy. The rebels of the NPFL moved from house to house, banged on people's doors, and broke down those doors that the people inside did not open. When they broke down the doors and entered the house, they summarily shot any occupants in the house. It was total confusion!

Our neighborhood became another trophy for Charles Taylor's forces, the National Patriotic Front of Liberia (NPFL), in their efforts to reach Central Monrovia. The NPFL was determined to capture Central Monrovia and President Samuel Doe before their rival break-away force, the Independent National Patriotic Front of Liberia (INPFL), led by Prince Johnson did. Prince Johnson had earlier had a dispute and separated with Charles Taylor over his authority as the self-proclaimed head of the National Patriotic Reconstruction Assembly Government (NPR), the alternative government to the Samuel Doe government, which was based in the Bong County town of Gbarnga. The NPFL rebels forced everyone out of their homes while they shot indiscriminately into the air. They also arrested and summarily executed civilians whom they suspected to have ties with the ruling government, the Krahn tribe (the tribe of President Doe), and Prince Johnson.

I think our mother might have already packed a small suitcase we had with some of our clothes, so as soon as she heard the banging on our door, and sensed that we might not be allowed back into our house, she picked up the suitcase, and we all stepped out with our hands in the air. That was one of the most frightening experiences I had ever had! Shortly afterward, the rebels assembled all the residents in that neighborhood onto an open field nearby, where we were all made to sit on the ground. Some of the leaders of that contingent went over and addressed us. They told us why they were fighting the government of President Doe and why they needed us all to cooperate with them to achieve that aim. They made us understand that they were fighting for the good of the nation and for security reasons, they were taking us to their Firestone camp, which was outside Monrovia. According to them, it was safer out there; they wanted to use the opportunity to flush out the "bad nuts" from among us and minimize the number of casualties when they launched their all-out assault on Central Monrovia. They just wanted to look good before us, so they told us all the nice things they could come up with. We were even made to shout chants in support of the revolution.

The NPFL rebel soldiers shot indiscriminately into the air, and many people were hit by stray bullets. After addressing us, we were marched to the Firestone camp, which was about twenty-eight miles from where we lived. On our way to the camp, the executions continued. As soon as someone was suspected to have ties with Samuel Doe's government, the Krahn tribe, the INPFL or showed any sign of resistance, they were pulled out of the exodus to Firestone and shot or beheaded. The beheadings were carried out with long machetes from the back of the victims' necks to make their death very excruciating. Some people had their limbs hacked off; some, their eyes gouged out; and others were beaten with rifles and left on the side of the road to die. People were tied to the backs of pickup trucks and dragged until they died. The journey was simply bloody, to say the least, and the aim was to put fear in us.

Our mother made sure we were on the move because the situation was very volatile. Just a hint of suspicion from one of the travelers to the rebel soldiers about another person led to that person's execution. Our journey was very long and arduous and lasted all day; the longest distance I have ever walked in my life. Our mother had just turned forty years old that April. We could not even celebrate her fortieth birthday because of the civil war. I was fourteen years old; my brother Peter was six years old; and Barbara, my sister, was seventeen months old. Occasionally, our mother allowed us to stop briefly to catch our breath, buy some finger foods, or pee. Mom used up all the money she had on her to buy a few finger foods on the way. The scenes of that day were so cruel that they are still vivid in my mind to this day. Those memories always make me emotional when they come to my mind. I still have those emotional scars with me to this day!

There were so many barriers/checkpoints on the way, and the rebel soldiers randomly stopped and searched anybody that looked suspicious. If they asked you a question and the answer you gave was not satisfactory, you were pulled out and beaten, shot, and/or executed. At some of the barriers, we saw human skulls, and at others, heads of people who had just been beheaded with their blood running down from the tables they were on. In some places, we came across the bodies of people who had been beaten and left to die or people who had been shot and their bodies left on the side of the road. Those scenes were very unpleasant for our little minds. I had never seen so much evil in my life. It felt like I had come face to face with the devil, and truly, I think the devil was working through those young men and women to carry out unimaginable evil.

In the next chapter, I will tell you about our arrival at the Firestone Camp and what life at the camp was like.

# Chapter 4

The Firestone Camp

We arrived at Firestone later that night very tired; our feet were seriously sore. Since we arrived at night, I didn't get a good look at the camp, but the scene was very chaotic. Almost everyone in that section of the camp was a newcomer, and they were all scrambling to find a place to "pitch their tent" for the night. Mom was given a place in a huge warehouse because she had three children. She took two big cloths from the suitcase we had on us, spread them on the cold concrete floor of the warehouse, and we laid right down and slept. I was so tired that I didn't remember anything after I laid down; I didn't even feel the hard cold floor I slept on until I woke up the next morning. The camp was very cold, and we were not prepared for it. What a sudden change that was! I just could not wrap my mind around the events of that day. We lost our freedoms! We turned into scavengers; eating any and everything we could find.

It was not until the next morning that I got a better view of the situation in the camp. The camp was huge, and there were very few buildings, but there were unending rows of rubber trees. I later found out that the camp was located on the reserve of Firestone Natural Rubber Limited Liability Company, a subsidiary of Bridgestone Americas Incorporated. The plantation was a huge real estate, almost the size of Chicago, and home to the largest rubber plantation in the world. I think that the plantation accounted for the cool microclimate in the camp. I also found out that the top leadership of the

National Patriotic Front of Liberia (NPFL) lived somewhere on the plantation, but I never saw any of them or where they lived.

People occupy every available space they could find in the camp—under trees, on sidewalks, in the warehouse, etc. The yard was dotted with so many makeshift tents. There were no doors and windows to the warehouse we slept in—all were broken. There was nothing like privacy in that camp, not even in the warehouse; anyone could just walk in and out of the warehouse at will. There were a few places designated as bathing areas for both genders, but people seldom bathed because it was really cold in the camp and there were more pressing needs than bathing. We did not bathe very often; sometimes just once a week, and even that was without any soap.

We stayed in that camp for about two and a half months, and those were the most disturbing months of my entire life. I don't wish that kind of life for anybody, not even my worst enemy! It felt like we lived in the jungle, under the supervision of animals. The militia went to our camp anytime they wanted. Executions were commonplace, and people were killed for no reason. I remember one Saturday afternoon, everybody was minding their own business when, out of nowhere, a group of armed young men, who were members of the militia, stormed into our yard, chanting: "I feel like killing!"

They went into the warehouse, randomly picked a man in his twenties, dragged him out of the warehouse, shot him, got into their vehicle, and drove off. I still remember the young man pleading, "Please have mercy on me! I have done nothing, please!"

But the young men did not care. I remember seeing flames from the rifle hitting the young man in his chest, and as he raised his hand to that part of his body, the second bullet hit his abdomen and he fell to his knees, then fell facedown. I remember the wife of the victim wailing as the young men who shot him sped off. It sent panic throughout the camp, and people started to find somewhere to hide because no one knew what was going to happen next. It was a very terrifying scene!

When I remember how girls and young women were treated, it sent shivers down my spine. It was really dangerous to be a young lady in those days. Parents with teenage girls were always on edge when members of the militia went to the camp; they hid their daughters wherever and however they could. Young ladies were forcibly seized, taken away, and gang-raped. One would always hear the pleads of those young ladies as they left. It was very frightening to watch! Some of the ladies were lucky to return alive. Those who returned alive came bleeding, and the experience was so traumatic that the victims were left in a bad physical, psychological, and sociological state. There were no proper systems in place to assist those girls; they always isolated themselves and wouldn't want to talk to anyone, not even their parents. I will not doubt that some of those girls may have even harmed themselves as a result of those experiences.

No one could freely walk around in the camp because you did not know when a group of young men from the militia would unleash a wave of mayhem on you. I remember once joining a group of boys on a farm to pick groundnuts. It was one of the days we were very hungry and I just needed to get something to eat. It was a bit far from the camp, and we even had to cross a fast-flowing river to get there. After about twenty to thirty minutes, we were surrounded by a group of young men of the militia. They said they had told us never to go to that farm to pick groundnuts, so they were going to kill all of us. I was frightened that day. I thought I was not going to see my family again. Thankfully, after threatening and keeping us for about an hour, they let us go. I was so relieved and vowed never to go out of the camp again!

The camp was littered with skeletal remains of decomposed bodies. The smell of the dead and putrefying flesh filled the air, and it was common to see ravens and vultures flying overhead and feeding on carrion. The stench was so awful that it was difficult to breathe when one got closer to the area. People who had asthma had frequent attacks; some people, especially children, even died. Once in a while, some brave young men organized themselves and went around the camp picking and burying dead bodies. It was that bad!

There was no food or clean drinking water in the camp. We drank water from any and every available source—streams, wells, and dug-out ponds. We scavenged any and everything we could find to eat: snails, crabs, fruits, nuts, cassava, and cassava leaves. The fruits, nuts, and new leaves of the tropical palm tree became a delicacy. People hunted for monkeys, birds, snakes, and many other animals. I remember coming across a tall palm tree in the bush on one of our scavenging expeditions. When my young brother and I found the palm nuts that day, it felt like we had found a lost gem. We were so excited! Due to the height of the tree and the prevailing civil war, no one climbed the tree to harvest the palm fruit. As such, the palm fruit got rotten on the tree, and when the branch could no longer hold it, it fell. We picked up two stones, sat there, cracked the nuts, and ate the nut to our fill. When our jaws were sore, we paused, opened our mouths wide for some few minutes, and just continued cracking and chewing the nuts. Yeah, it was that bad!

The dense vegetation in the camp created suitable breeding conditions for insects and other bugs, and there were many plants that people could eat. People developed all kinds of ailments—skin rashes, diarrhea—and many others died after eating poisonous plants. I had a lot of skin rashes due to the incessant insect bites, not bathing regularly, or eating healthy food. We regularly heard the screams and laments of desperate mothers whose children were dying. There were no clinics, hospitals, or pharmacies to get medication. If someone was ill and their immune system was not strong enough to keep them alive, they just drop dead. Life in that camp was a nightmare. I remember fainting on one occasion after puffing into a fire I was trying to light to boil some large snails I gathered earlier that evening. Fortunately, my mother was very close by, and she quickly picked me up, poured some water on me, and I came around. My brother and I made a sport out of counting our ribs because we had grown very thin; we looked like skeletons!

The young men of the militia were always in the camp. They wore talismans around their necks, wigs, grotesque masks, and rubber sandals, and were always high on drugs. The talismans appeared to be made from feathers, human bones, and other items, which they believed protected them from bullets and gave them a sense of security, invincibility, and reckless boldness. Children as young as nine years old were recruited into the militia. Often when they told stories of why they joined the insurgency, it frightened you. Almost all of them were forcefully recruited. Some of them had their entire family murdered before them and were given the option of either joining the militia or suffering the same fate as their family. They told these stories while brutalizing or killing someone. Often armed with AK-47s, long machetes, and other assorted rifles, these child soldiers were the most violent and devoted of all, unleashing mayhem everywhere they went. These boys became extremely wicked, the personification of evil.

Teenagers and young men were mostly the commanders of smaller units. They were the ones carrying the rocket-propelled grenade launchers and other artilleries. These unit commanders drove their teams around and led new assaults. They were also fearless and vicious. They carried out beheadings and other related executions. You dare not challenge them; they acted before they thought. These rebel soldiers moved in groups, either in stolen cars or pickup trucks. Robbing people was normal. They always announced their presence with a lot of noise and indiscriminate firing in the air. Different groups went into the camp at different times. Somebody always died or a young girl got kidnapped before they left. The camp was like a playground for them and the people, their toys.

In the next section, I will tell you about how we escaped from the Firestone and how life outside the camp turned out.

Chapter 5

The Escape

Life in the camp was a nightmare, and Mom was not comfortable with it at all. She was worried that what we were seeing might have a long-term negative impact on our development. She was always on the lookout and regularly sought opportunities to get us out of the camp. Sometime in early August 1990, after a long thorough assessment of the situation, Mom found out that Sundays were a good day to travel out of the camp because the militias used the day to rest, clean their weapons, and strategize for the week ahead. Mom conceived the idea of sneaking out of the camp to find out whether our neighborhood, New Matadi Estate, was safe and habitable for us to leave the camp because we lived in constant danger. She had heard from some people in the camp that people who had returned were living a fairly comfortable life as compared to those of us at the Firestone camp.

The day our mother decided to sneak out of the camp, she rose very early that morning to be able to return before nightfall. I could not go scavenging for food as was my regular practice because I had to stay around and take care of my siblings. She told one of the families we had befriended in the camp to keep an eye on us. She was away for the entire day and returned a little later that evening. She brought news that life was much better outside the camp, although we did not have a home to return to. Our house had been ransacked and all our belongings carried away. All our pictures and other valuable documents had either been looted or destroyed. The only glimmer of hope she had was her Songhai sewing machine she found hidden somewhere at our house, which the looters had not seen. She planned that when we were fortunate to return, we would go and bring it back with us. According to our mother, she would sew for people in our neighborhood to earn some money for our upkeep. She could sew all kinds of clothes—for both males and females—she even made all our clothes, so I knew it was a good idea.

According to Mom, she also went to Gardnersville (or Gardnesville), the suburb in which Golden Age International, the elementary school she managed, was located. She was fortunate to find that the school's custodian, who lived about a block away, still lived in his house. She was given access to the building and found the school intact and somewhat habitable because all the mattresses the preschoolers and kindergarteners napped on were still there. The custodian was also willing to give her the keys to the building and allow us to live there temporarily. The custodian also assured her that it was okay and safe for us to live in the school because there were very few disturbances in the community. Besides, the owner of the school, who was a Ghanaian, had returned to Ghana when the crisis was getting worse. Our mother, therefore, decided that instead of returning to our house at New Matadi Estate or staying at the camp in the Firestone plantation where our lives were at risk—and there was nothing to sleep on—we would go and stay at the elementary school and use the mattresses there and be closer to town.

Mom also said she interacted with some people on her journey to and from town, and they confirmed that Sundays were the best days to travel that road because the militia rested and held their strategic meetings, and as such, there were few of the men along the roads and very little or no harassments. She, therefore, planned we would leave the camp the following week. On Sunday, August 26, 1990, we left the camp and started the forty-six-kilometer journey back to the school. Along the way, we met a man who was a member of the militia, driving a pickup truck headed in our direction. He gave us a ride in the bucket of his truck. It was such a welcome relief for us because I was dreading that long walk to town. The young man got to us at the right time; we had started to feel the heat of the sun as the sun was high in the sky. We were hungry and very tired from the long walk.

The young man dropped us off at a point where we only had to walk for about thirty minutes to get to the school premises at Gardnersville. It was such a great relief, and we were so grateful to the young man. When we arrived, our mom went to the custodian's house and took the keys, and we went in and lodged in one of the classrooms. The building was very huge, and I still remember the smell in the building. It smelt like an old wooden box stack some-where in an abandoned attic that had not been opened for a long time. When Mom sneaked out of the camp the previous weekend, she met some friends who gave her some uncooked rice. That allowed us to have some food to eat throughout that week.

We had a long rest that night, and we woke up very late the following afternoon, Monday. We did not really do much that day, but stayed indoors the entire day and took things easy. It was such a delight to have some relief from our terrible life in the Firestone camp. However, two days after we arrived in town, the rice ran out. I remember for dinner on Tuesday night, we could only get a handful of cooked rice. After we ate ours, we told our mother we were not full, so she gave us her portion of rice, and she slept on an empty stomach. I still have that scene engraved in my mind! What a selfless mother Dorothy was to us. She will forever have a special place in my heart!

Shortly after our meal that evening, our mother suggested we should go to our house the following morning, Wednesday, August 29, to bring her Songhai sewing machine. I agreed. But when I thought about it for a while, I asked our mother, "Where will you leave Peter and Barbara?"

"I will speak to the caretaker in the morning. I am sure he wouldn't mind them spending a few hours with him and his family while we are away," she replied. "He lives at the other end of that block," she added as she pointed to a block nearby.

"But they do not know him, so I am not sure they will be com-fortable staying with him," I stated. "Why don't I rather stay with

Barbara and you go with Peter instead. I can take care of Barbara, rather than they staying with a stranger," I added.

After discussing the idea for a while, our mother realized that my idea was better. So she agreed, and we got ready to retire for the night. That night, our mother did something strange. It was strange to me because I had never seen her nor remember her ever doing that. She read a passage in the Psalms from Gideon's International New Testament Pocket Size King James Bible. I cannot recall the particular Psalm she read, but I remember it was one of those Psalms David prayed, I guess, in his time of distress. After she was done reading the Psalm, she prayed over us. I was dozing off when she was praying, but I remember she prayed with such intensity, an intensity that I have never seen before.

As stated earlier, everything she did that night was new to me, so I didn't really wrap my mind around it. It was unusual because we were not a praying family. Maybe my mother used to pray, but I don't remember. It felt like our mother had sensed something was going to happen. My mother was a strong woman, the rock of the family, and up until that point, she had shown no sign of fear or panic—she was our rock—but that night was very different. She cried out to God! She asked for forgiveness for all her sins, and her mistakes, and prayed that God will keep us safe! When she was done, I said my feeble, sleepy "Amen" and slept. All through that night, Mother was restless, and she could just not sleep. She woke me up a couple of times. I even remember her telling me she was afraid and thought something had happened or something was going to happen. She just couldn't tell why she was feeling that way. I remember telling her that everything was going to be okay and that she should not worry because I will be there to help her.

It rained heavily all through the night, with lightning flashes and thunders. I remember it was still raining heavily that morning, Wednesday, August 29, 1990, when Mom woke me up to lock the door as she and Peter were ready to leave. I asked her to wait a while because it was still raining, but she insisted it was getting late and that she wanted to return before nightfall. Unknown to me, they had been waiting for so long, and the rain was not subsiding. The journey was also very long, and it was going to take them over an hour to get to our house at New Matadi Estate. They did not have breakfast that morning because there was nothing in the house to eat. Unlike in the camp where I could go scavenge something from the plantation for us to eat, there was practically no vegetation to glean something from. We had eaten our last meal the previous night. Unfortunately for me, I did not even see my brother that morning before they left. I barely looked into Mom's eyes that morning when she asked me to go lock the door. I was still sleepy; I just said my feeble, "Bye, Mom," and went back to sleep beside Barbara, who was still fast asleep. Unknowingly, that was my final goodbye to our mother and brother!

I was later awakened by my sister when she wanted to use the bathroom. The first question she asked me when I woke up was, "Where is Mom?"

I told her she had gone to get our sewing machine, and she will soon be back. We waited all day for our mother and brother, but they never showed up. That day was very tough for me. My sister kept asking when our mother would return. I had to even sit by the window to the main entrance of the building with my sister on my lap all day, just to assure her that our mom and brother would return and to keep her calm. Toward the evening, I became very anxious and scared. Our mother had never left us all alone for that long, and it was very hard for me to grapple with the thought that she had not returned.

The thought of spending the night without my mother was frightening for me. My sister was very hungry and restless, and she kept bothering me. We, however, managed to fall asleep that night. Sometime later that night, my sister woke up and wanted to nurse because she was very hungry. When she realized that our mother had still not returned, she started to cry. I did all I could to keep her calm, but nothing worked; she just kept on crying. I was afraid that a passerby would hear us and try to harm us. After trying all I could to let her stop crying and nothing worked, I joined her and we cried ourselves back to sleep.

The next morning, that was Thursday, my sister and I woke up unusually early. We did not know anyone in the neighborhood nor did we have anywhere to go. I decided to go to the school custodian's house and tell him about our ordeal and the failure of our mother to return after she left for town. He sympathized with us and told us that we could spend the day with his family. Luckily, he had some food, so we had something to eat that day. I was very anxious that day, and I kept peeking in the direction of the school just to ensure that I did not miss Mom and my brother when they returned, but she never showed up that day also.

I was losing it; I could not hold myself together. I just could not come up with any possible explanation why Mother had still not shown up. I had had worse experiences up to that point, but none of them was comparable to what I experienced in those two days; it was just unbearable! Later that evening, we returned to the school to sleep. That night I took the Gideon's Bible that Mother read from that Tuesday night and tried to look for the prayer she prayed over us, but I did not find it because I did not take note of the chapter and verse. I felt that I needed to pray, but I did not know how to pray, what to pray about, and whom to pray to. I simply cried myself to sleep.

We woke up a little late that morning, and when we showed up at the custodian's house that Friday, he was not amused at all. He was very hostile to us! Our presence meant two extra mouths to feed for another day, but I do not blame him because he did not have the means to continually feed us. He was the only person we knew in that neighborhood so we could not go to anyone but him. He did not even welcome us into his house that day, so we spent the day outside, under a tree near the house. They hid their food from us from that day; I suspect they got up very early and ate before we got to his house that morning, and they did not show any sign of preparing food or eating that entire day. My sister and I ate nothing that day. I think they ate later that evening when we returned to the school premises to sleep.

Apart from that, the custodian spoke very badly about our mother and that got me very angry at him. He alleged that our mother was incapable of caring for us so she used the sewing machine as an excuse just to abandon us and run away. I felt it was my duty to defend my mother, and I did so to the best of my ability, but his words triggered a lot of thoughts in my mind. I knew the sacrifices our mother had made for us up until that point, how she loved us, and the hardships she had endured for us. I made him understand that she loved us and that she would not abandon us for anything in the world. I kept telling him maybe something had held them up and that they would certainly return. He did not care; he just wanted us out! His nasty comments caused me not to go near his house, but he would intentionally go to where I sat and say something hurtful about my mother.

After every few minutes, he would go to where we sat and pass an irritating comment or two about our mother. One of the comments that got under my skin and caused me to decide to do something about my situation was when he went over to us and said, "You just can't sit here doing nothing. You need to go find your mother because she isn't coming back. Go find her!"

There was such a mean look on his face when he made that comment, and I sarcastically replied, "I will go find my mother tomorrow morning." The following day was a Saturday, exactly three days after our mother left us and did not return.

"Good!" he responded as he walked away.

When the custodian left, I began to feel the weight of what I had just said. I was suddenly overpowered by fear; my heartbeat increased, and I lost the little strength I had left. It felt like I had mistakenly gone to pick a fight with the big fat bully in my school, and he was going to get me. It felt like the bully gave me that look that says something like, "You are a dead man!" I became very worried. I didn't know what I was going to do. I felt the custodian had succeeded in making my life complicated. I sat under the tree for a while and just decided to leave. I went over to the entrance of his house and called out to him that we were returning to the school premises, and he replied without going out of his room. I turned and left because I did not want to hear any more of his rants; I just wanted to be alone to clear my mind.

I had no idea where to start my search. I needed to have a plan and I needed it fast. We did not have internet in those days. I didn't have a map of New Matadi Estate nor did I know how to get there. I was very restless that evening. But I resolved to go and find my mother no matter what the consequences would be. I couldn't go sit around and not know what had happened to my mother and brother. I was confused, and the uncertainty was killing me. It felt like I was stuck in a huge quagmire and did not know how to pull myself out.

I could also not discuss my decision with anyone because I didn't know anybody in the neighborhood. I was alone and afraid! When I could not bear it anymore, I picked up Gideon's New Testament Bible and tried to find the verse of Scripture our mother prayed with that faithful night, but for the third time, I did not find it. It felt like that verse of Scripture had also given up on me and vanished from the pages of the Bible. I closed the Bible and tried to pray, but I couldn't get a single word out of my mouth; I just wailed! My sister just laid there staring at me, hungry and helpless. Somehow, we both fell asleep.

In the next chapter, I will tell you about the events of Saturday, September 1, 1990—the day I decided that I would go find my mother.

CHAPTER 6

The Perilous Journey

Sometime that night, I was awakened by heavy sporadic shootings and the shelling of artilleries. Rising slightly from the floor—I had learned never to stand up when there were shooting—I peeked through the window and saw huge balls of fire overhead, one after another, moving in the direction of central Monrovia. When they fell, the ground shook and the windows rattled. The fighting was very intense and frightening! I thought to myself, *Maybe we should go and sleep in the kitchen instead because it is smaller and there were many cabinets there we could hide in. When someone went into the building the last place they would like to look for a human being would be in the kitchen cabinet.*

I quickly picked my sister up onto my shoulder, picked up the mattress we were sleeping on, and dashed across the dark hallway toward the kitchen. As I ran to the kitchen, I asked myself, *Why is there a sudden escalation in fighting? Everything seemed calm and normal the previous day.*

As soon as we got into the kitchen and laid down, I realized after a few seconds that there were so many mosquitoes in there. I could hear the buzzing sound of the mosquitoes. The gunshots were intense, and the mosquitoes were feasting on us. I had seen people and heard stories about people who had been hit by stray bullets while standing or walking, even in their homes. I therefore decided to just stay put in the kitchen despite the mosquito bites because returning to the classroom was risky for us. We simply stayed in the kitchen and endured the mosquito bites. We could not sleep for the rest of the night. The battle continued throughout the night into the wee hours of the morning. It felt like the shootings were taking place just behind the school building. After all, mosquitoes and ant bites were not new to us. We had just returned from the Firestone Camp, where we were food for the insects and where we slept on the cold floor with only a layer of cloth under us.

Just when we started to see glimpses of the morning light, the fighting subsided and we were able to get some sleep. When I woke up in the morning, I laid down for a while to assess the situation before getting up. The neighborhood was silent; not even the buzz of the mosquitoes could be heard. Sensing that things were calm, I got up and tiptoed around to find out whether everything was okay. For the first time, I felt insecure in the school building. That was when I noticed that there was some stagnant water in the kitchen sink that had bred mosquitoes. I uncorked it and allowed the water to drain out. I also noticed so many bite marks and sores all over our bodies as a result of the incessant bites and scratches. Barbara's eyes were also swollen as a result of the mosquito bites, but that was the least of my troubles that day. I was stepping out of the security of the school building into an unknown world, and that thought scared me to my bones. I had no other alternatives; I just had to do what I had to do that day! That morning was Saturday, September 1, 1990, and what a way to start a new month that was?

My sister was not feeling good that morning; she whined from the time she woke up until it was time for us to leave. She did not have a good night's sleep, and to make matters worse, she was very hungry. We did not eat the previous day because the custodian hid his food from us. She was still crying when we went out of the school building. I set her down on the ground, and in protest, she sat on the ground. At that point, I thought to myself, *I don't think I can carry Barbara with me on this journey because it will be a very long walk, and because of the way she is crying, it will be very difficult to carry her. Maybe I should just leave her with the custodian. More so, we are both very sick and weak from the prolonged period of starvation.*

As I thought about that idea, I remembered one of the many pieces of advice my mother gave me: "Always think about the effect of your actions on the people around you because your actions will not only impact you but the people you love as well." So I did! I asked myself, *What if something happened to me on the way and I was unable to return for Barbara, what will happen to her? What if during my wandering, I met my mother and she asked where I had left her only daughter? What explanation would I have for leaving Barbara behind?*

Just then, I heard a voice asking me, "You promised to take care of your sister in Mom's absence?"

"Yes!" I responded.

"Then, just do so because Sister [our mother] will not be happy if you leave her daughter behind," the voice whispered again to me. Just then, the image of my mother's face when she was disappointed about something I had done came into my mind. After that dialogue with myself and that voice, I remembered that there are a lot of rumors of people kidnapping and selling children for rituals. That particular thought sent chills down my spine, and I vowed that I will not leave my only sister because I did not want her to be used for ritual, despite the difficulties I may encounter. I picked Barbara up from the floor, wiped her tears, and comforted her as we went back into the school building to pick up our things for the journey.

I took the New Testament Bible and put it in my left pocket. Although I had opened it a couple of times to find the Psalm our mother read that Tuesday night, I did not find it. So I just kept it. I honestly did not have the peace of mind to read it. I put my sister on my back, and we went to the custodian's house to say goodbye before leaving. On the way, I don't remember who it was, but a man gave me a twenty-Liberian-dollar coin. There was nothing much we could buy with it, but I accepted it and put it in my right pocket. As we walked away from our neighborhood, we bought a piece of sugarcane from a boy whom I found selling along the path we were walking on. The sugarcane was a little longer than two inches, but that was the only thing edible we could buy with it. I remember telling Barbara, who by then stopped crying, "I will keep it in my pocket until we are very hungry, then we will eat it."

She just said, "Okay."

As we walked on, I kept assuring her that we would find Mom very soon, and everything will be okay, but she did not say much, just quietly listened to me.

Our Arrest

Barbara and I walked in the direction of our former neighborhood at New Matadi Estate. I simply relied on my little knowledge of geography and bearings at that time. We walked past two checkpoints that were unmanned, probably because it was still early. About thirty minutes into our journey, I saw another checkpoint in the distance. As we drew closer, I noticed a middle-aged Liberian man walking ahead of us, and he got to the checkpoint before us. When we got to the checkpoint, I noticed a boy soldier, whom I assume was between nine to eleven years old, holding an AK-47 assault rifle. He was the one manning that checkpoint and judging by his appearance, he was one of those heartless boy soldiers of the NPFL I described in my earlier chapter. He had this mean look on his face; like someone who did not want to be out there so early that morning. The boy stopped the man, searched him and his baggage, and asked him which Liberian tribe he belonged to.

"Bassa," he replied. Bassa is one of the sixteen ethnic groups in Liberia. Fortunately for him, he did not belong to President Doe's tribe nor did he come from any of the enemy tribes, so the boy soldier beckoned the man to go.

When he got to me, I wanted to also say I was Bassa, but something told me, "You are a Ghanaian, so, tell the truth." That was also one of the many pieces of advice my mother gave me. Mom taught me to "always tell the truth, even if it will cost you your life."

Just then I responded, "I am a Ghanaian."

"Oh!" the boy screamed, "you are the people we are looking for. You damn foreigner! Your people are not allowing this thing to end. I will deal with you today."

I honestly did not know what he was talking about. He cocked his gun and ordered, "Move!"

Knowing what these child soldiers were capable of doing, I just followed his orders. I just could not figure out why it had become a crime to be a Ghanaian living in Liberia.

I later found out that around the time, the sixteen-member Economic Community of West African States (ECOWAS) had deployed a joint military intervention force known as ECOMOG (The Economic Community Monitoring Group) to Monrovia under a Nigerian leadership. Their objectives were to impose a cease-fire and help Liberians establish an interim government until elections could be held; stop the killing of innocent civilians and ensure the safe evacuation of foreign nationals; and prevent the conflict from spreading into neighboring countries.[1] The ECOMOG forces arrived at the Freeport of Monrovia on August 24, 1990—five days before the day our mother went missing—and they were moving inland.

Parts of Central Monrovia had already fallen to and were under the control of Prince Johnson, a former NPFL fighter/leader who broke away to form his guerrilla force, the Independent National Patriotic Front of Liberia (INPFL). Charles Taylor's militia was working earnestly to reach Central Monrovia, so the arrival of ECOMOG was a serious setback to their efforts. I guess that explains the heavy fighting that occurred the previous night. This enraged Charles Taylor and his men, causing them to misplace their anger on all foreign nationals living in the country, especially those from the other West African States. I remember the militia rounding up and executing foreign nationals—Nigerians, Ghanaians, Guineans, etc.—who lived in Liberia at the time, but it did not make sense to me.

The boy soldier led me and my sister to his unit commander, who was stationed about a mile away from where we were arrested. On our way, I took out the sugarcane from my pocket and ate with Barbara. I thought to myself, *I know that I am done. I have never seen anyone who had gotten to this point and survived. Why should I be killed without eating my sugarcane? If they decide to kill us, we will at least have something in our stomachs.*

---

[1] "First Liberian Civil War," Wikipedia, accessed April 13, 2020, https://en.wikipedia.org/wiki/First_Liberian_Civil_War.

When we arrived at the unit commander's station, the commander was a young man, probably in his early twenties. He was in the company of some young men and women and having a lot of fun. They were on a drinking spree; drinking a lot of alcoholic beverages and smoking marijuana. The air around them was filled with smoke; it was intoxicating. One particular beverage that I remember seeing was Gordon's London dry gin. I noticed that liquor because several empty bottles laid around, and the bottles that were not empty were on a small table in front of them. They were making loud noises, and no one dared ask them to tone down. I suspected they might have looted a liquor store sometime earlier and were feasting on their booty.

When I saw the scene, I became terrified! I could feel my heart pounding hard in my chest. I was familiar with that scene, the scene of total madness, death, and destruction. I just knew my end had come, and I was paralyzed by fear! I could hardly swallow my saliva—it felt like I was swallowing a huge ball of something. We had finished eating our sugarcane by then, and I braced myself for the worst.

The boy soldier went to his unit commander, bent over, and whispered into his ears. I don't know what he told him, but I assumed he might have told him something to the effect that we were Ghanaians. As soon as the unit commander heard whatever he was told, he jumped out of his seat, staggered toward his rifle, which lay about two feet away from where he sat, cocked it, and ordered, "Give me six feet!"

"Giving six feet" was one of the many jargons I had heard many times at the Firestone Camp, so I knew what he meant. I quickly backed away and walked for a few more feet. As he raised his rifle to aim at me, I heard him shout, "Stop right there!"

At that point, I lost my breath and I felt that I had been enveloped by a wind of terror. I gave up on life at that point. I was just tired of the pain and suffering. I just wanted everything to end! I could no longer bear the sense of hopelessness. I just could not go on with life anymore.

When my sister saw what was going on, she started screaming. Her screams were so deafening that they woke me up from unconsciousness. Out of the screams, I heard the unit commander ordering me "Put the little girl down! Put the little girl down!"

When my sister heard that, she held tightly onto me. I couldn't get her to leave me! I don't know where she got that strength from. My sister's screams grew even louder! I also felt my heart beating heavily.

Suddenly, a man appeared standing beside the unit commander and was talking with him. At that point, we had moved out of the view of the group we saw when we arrived. I didn't see him when we arrived on the scene and he didn't appear intoxicated as the others were. It was strange to me because I didn't see him walking toward the commander either. If he had come from the direction of the group, I would have surely seen him. Moreover, the area was bushy and enclosed, and there was only one way to get there—the direction we had come from. There was no way this stranger could have walked onto the scene without me noticing him.

He spoke to the commander as if they were childhood friends, freely and casually. This stranger distracted the commander with so many questions to the point that he couldn't focus on shooting us. From what I have seen up until that point, these young militiamen were vicious and strong-willed; once they made up their minds to kill someone, no amount of pleas or anyone could talk them out of it. But this stranger was able to talk the commander out of killing us. It happened so fast that I couldn't understand what was going on. Initially, I taught it was a dream. I don't know, but it felt like I had left my body at a point. I just stood there speechless and overwhelmed by fear. Looking back on that event, I realize that fear is a very paralyzing force; it can kill a person instantly.

The part of their dialogue that I overheard was:

The stranger: "What do you want to do to this boy?

The commander: "I want to kill this *f——king* Ghanaian."

The stranger: "You should not kill him because he is the one taking care of this little girl?"

The commander: "I don't care."

The stranger: "But If you kill him, who is going to take care of this little girl? Do you want to kill her also?"

The commander: "No, I will not kill her, I will send her to my wife in the village to take care of her."

The stranger: "I don't think your wife will want to take care of a little girl who cries this much! You better let these children go because this girl will give your wife a hard time if you kill her brother."

At this point, my sister was screaming at the top of her lungs. It was very loud and irritating. My sister was not a crybaby, so her behavior that day really surprised me! The stranger persisted until the commander finally lowered his rifle, disengaged it, and calmed down.

The commander then turned to me and asked, "Where are you going?"

"I am going to look for our mother who left us three days ago but had not returned," I replied.

"Was she with a little boy?" he asked.

"Yes," I answered.

"I killed them," he answered with a kind of gratification and arrogance. "I shot both of them over there," he said, pointing to some shrubs nearby.

"Do you want to see their bodies? They are still laying there; we have not buried them yet."

Out of fear, I said, "No."

When I heard that he had killed our mother, my heart sunk. It felt like a dagger had been thrust through my heart. I wanted to cry, but I held it back and showed no emotions. I was afraid that the commander might change his mind if I had shown any emotions or if I had agreed to see the lifeless bodies of our mother and brother, particularly in his present state of mind—intoxicated. Again, I did not want to see my dear mother laying out there in a humiliated state. I knew that scene was going to haunt me forever. It felt like I was having a nightmare only to realize that I was not dreaming at all. It was too much to bear. I was so disoriented by his statement that I just stood there like a zombie!

At that point, I was convinced that the worse had happened to my mother and brother. As the oldest child, I knew our mother loved us so much and would not leave us for three days if nothing had happened to her. She would never, ever, for any reason in the world, abandon us for three days. No way! We were so dear to her. Our mother worked very hard to make sure we were okay. She was tireless! Although I have somewhat healed, I still feel the pain, like touching the scar of a deep wound!

The commander then turned and told me, "Return to where you are coming from. It is much safer there. You will be killed if you go any further."

Yeah, you guessed rightly! The commander who was under the influence of drugs and alcohol was advising me! He just told me I would be killed if I continued my journey.

The commander then asked me, "Have you eaten today?"

"No," I responded.

He added, "When I give you some food, will you be able to cook it?"

"Yes," I said.

He then turned to the boy soldier who arrested us and had just joined us there and said, "Go to the storehouse and give them some rice."

The thought of walking away free and getting some food after starving for two days was reassuring. I was convinced that the troubles of that day were over, not knowing the boy soldier was not happy about his unit commander's decision to let us go free.

As soon as we left the commander's presence, the boy soldier turned and asked me, "Do you want rice or do you want your life?" vigorously lifting and motioning his rifle in my face with a mean look. The boy really wanted us dead! I am sure his day did not start well, and he wanted to have us killed to appease himself. As mentioned earlier, these child soldiers had no sense of pity or mercy, therefore when I realized what his intentions were, I just turned without saying a word and walked away.

I never got to mourn my parents; I never said goodbye to my beloved mother and brother! I have tried to forget those events of 1990, but it has become a part of my life. That day, my whole world crumbled! My hopes, dreams, and all the plans we had as a family vanished! I just knew life would never be the same again. My mother was my world! I was hit with the harsh reality that my sister and I were all alone in this life.

What am I going to do now? I thought to myself as we walked back to the elementary school we stayed at. *Where am I going? Who is going to take care of us?* We did not know anybody in that neighborhood apart from the custodian, but he also did not want to have anything to do with us. I was totally lost in my thoughts!

That was not the end of the day's events. In the next chapter, I will tell you what happened to us when we were just about 200 feet away from the elementary school.

CHAPTER 7

A Breath of Hope

On our way back, I asked my sister, "Why were you screaming so hard?" What she told me blew my mind.

"I thought the man with the gun said you should put me down so he could shoot me. I didn't want to die, so I started screaming," she replied.

It became clear to me that she was aware of what was happening. I am sure she even saw some of the executions because they happened so frequently that they could not be hidden! Our mother tried her best to prevent us from seeing the many terrible things by telling us not to look at them, but it was just not possible. The executions were very frequent as we traveled to Firestone and while we lived in the camp. Well, if I had not seen them, how would I have been able to tell this story?

That experience and the advice of the unit commander really frightened me. For that reason, I stayed away from the footpaths and the main road on our way back because there were checkpoints and barriers all along the way. Although I had safely gone through those same checkpoints earlier that morning, I was not sure that I was going to get through them easily on our way back. I found a stick, and I pretended to be scavenging for food as I walked back to the school. I did not want anybody to suspect us or stop and question us. Whenever I saw someone approaching or looking in our direction, I would stop and pretend to be looking for something in the bushes.

I was shaken by the experience! All this while, I carried my sister on my back and supported her with one hand, and held the stick in the other hand. I switched hands when I felt tired of supporting her with that hand.

About a block away from the school, I found a footpath that went toward a soccer field. In the distance, I realized that the path went between two houses in the direction of the school. I decided to use that path. As soon as I got out of the bushes and stepped onto that footpath, the temperature suddenly dropped. It felt like the heavens opened and it started to rain. I threw the stick away, and held my sister with both hands as I tried to walk a little faster to avoid getting soaked in the rain. We did not have many changing clothes, so I did not want us to get wet.

As we approached the two houses, I saw two women leaning against the rail of the porch of one of the houses chatting. I later got to know that it was a woman and her daughter. I greeted them. Then the woman, named Maa Nuva, as we got to know later, asked me, "Where are you coming from in this rain?"

Just then my sister turned to look at the person speaking. Maa Nuva noticed her swollen eyelids and exclaimed, "And what happened to the little girl's eyes?"

My sister's eyes did not look good at all; she could barely open them. Apart from that, we looked like walking skeletons. I started to tell her about our ordeal. I did not even get halfway through our story then Maa Nuva became emotional. She didn't even allow me to complete my story. At a point, I even felt sorry for telling her. She said she had noticed that people were living in the school, but she could not pry because it was risky. The land around the school was a little elevated, so it could easily be noticed when there was an activity in and around the school.

Maa Nuva then asked me, "Have you eaten today?"

"No," I responded.

"Do you know how to cook?" she added.

"Yes, I can," I answered.

"That's good because I do not have any cooked food in the house right now, we have already eaten for the day," she stated. I did not have any means of telling the time, but I guess it must have been around 4:00 p.m. because the sun had moved westward, toward the direction of the sunset before it started to rain.

Maa Nuva asked her daughter to bring us a bench for us to sit on as she motioned us to get out of the rain onto the porch. She quickly went into her house and brought us some rice, a little pan to cook in, a tin of sardines, some charcoal, and a box of matches. She even wanted to give us a coal pot (a cooking device usually made from aluminum), but I told her we had one at the school.

Then she added, "If you would not mind, you could go to live with me when you are done with your food. At least you will have something to eat and have some peace of mind after all you have been through this week." I told her I will love to stay with her and thanked her as we left. By then, the rain had stopped.

I was so excited, and for a while, I forgot about the horrific and painful experience I had had that day and looked forward to eating some good food. That was my third miracle that day! The boy soldier and his commander did not kill me, my life was not endangered by going closer to central Monrovia, and here I was with food to eat that evening. We were not supposed to sleep hungry that night and by divine providence, we did not. Although one door closed before us earlier that day—when the boy soldier refused to give us food from their storage—God provided us a meal packaged in compassion!

Like my mother would have wanted me to do, I thought that I should take the food to the caretaker's house and cook it there, so we could all eat, but when I got there, I found the caretaker's lifeless body lying in the bushes nearby and his house ransacked. I did not find any member of his family around either. That was when the enormity of the decision I took that morning hit me. I realized that taking my sister along with me was the best decision I made. I began to think to myself, *what would have happened to me if I had left my sister behind? I would have lost my life that day, but for her screams! What would have also happened to my sister when the custodian's family was attacked?*

From that moment onward, I began to value the many pieces of advice my mother gave me. Her wise words and good training had saved our lives. That day, I vowed never to leave my sister with anyone because she was the only family I had in Liberia.

I stood at the custodian's house for a little while, totally lost in my thoughts. When my thoughts had run their full course, we returned to the elementary school premises. I just could not make sense of what happened to us that day! When I got to the premises, I quickly lit the fire, cooked the rice, and together, my sister and I ate to our fill. It was a real feast we had that evening. After we were done with the meal, we laid down to rest, but we did not wake up until the following morning. I didn't even lock the doors that night!

I picked up our little suitcase as soon as we woke up that morning and went straight to Maa Nuva's house. She was very excited to see us. She thought something had happened to us when we did not show up the previous evening. We stayed with her for about three weeks, and Maa Nuva took very good care of us. She helped us forget about all our pains and sufferings for the entire period we lived with her. She was God-sent; she even discussed plans for helping me get back into school when the war ended. She stepped into the big shoes of our mother pretty well. I am so thankful for that lady because she restored some hope to my broken life!

All through those challenging times, I never had a single nightmare, not even a dream of our mother. It was like our fragile minds were shielded from all the horrors we saw and the heart-wrenching experiences we had. I could have gotten depressed or even gone insane by all the evils I witnessed. Our souls and spirits were shielded from the damaging effects of those events.

I was in Maa Nuva's house on the morning of September 9, 1990, when we heard an uproar of jubilations echoing from the direction of Freeport. We later learned that President Doe had been captured by the forces of Prince Johnson. "The Monkey," as the Liberians referred to President Doe, had fallen.

That day, I heard the forces of INPFL chanting, "Monkey come down, heo, heo, heo, Monkey come down heo!" The chanting, singing, and a few sporadic gunshots went on for a few minutes before ending abruptly. The death of President Doe did not bring any calm to the situation in Monrovia. The NPFL's struggle for the control of Central Monrovia continued because Charles Taylor was very obsessed with the idea of taking over Liberia. The entry of the Economic Community Monitoring Group (ECOMOG), however, brought some order into Monrovia. ECOMOG gradually pushed back the NPFL rebels and gained enough ground to evacuate most of the foreign nationals still in the country.

In the next chapter, I will tell you about how the Ghanaian contingent of ECOMOG found my sister and me and how we finally made the journey back to Ghana.

CHAPTER 8

The Rescue

Sometime toward the end of September 1990, ECOMOG (the West African Peace Keeping Force) pushed Charles Taylor's militias further back into the outskirts of Monrovia and took over our neighborhood. The takeover went by almost unnoticed, although there were a few sporadic gunshots but not a full-fledged battle as we previously knew accompanied military takeovers. We woke up one morning just to find several armored vehicles driving through the major streets of Gardnersville. We heard a few scattered gunshots, and before long, we saw the Nigerian ground troops patrolling our neighborhood. After a few days, the Nigerian contingent was replaced by a different set of uniformed men.

As I brushed my teeth outside that morning, I noticed that these soldiers were moving around from house to house, chatting with people in the neighborhood. They asked people how they were doing and whether there had been any disturbances in the neighborhood in the past few days. They were just making sure the NPFL rebels had all left the community and people were safe. After brushing my teeth, I quickly went inside to put my toothbrush down and went back outside to take a close look at these new soldiers I had seen. I noticed that they were wearing badges that had the flag of Ghana.

When I realized that they were Ghanaians, I started to look for an opportunity to speak to one of them. I had not spoken to any of them, but I thought the best way I could get their attention was to speak to them in Twi, a common Ghanaian language. I thought to myself, *Maybe if I spoke a Ghanaian language, they would know that I am truly a Ghanaian.*

I was just excited to see Ghanaians around. I did not think about the implication of me speaking to them. Our parents had stopped speaking our Ghanaian language at home with us because they wanted us to learn to speak the English language fluently to fully integrate into the Liberian society. Our mother was from Larteh in the Eastern Region of Ghana, so we used to speak Twi at home. They only spoke Twi to us when they wanted to tell us something that they did not want people around to understand. Around that time, there were a lot of hostilities toward foreign nationals living in Liberia, so I guess our parents stopped speaking our local language with us to disguise our nationality. The foreigners were dominating the job market in Liberia and were making more money than the Liberians. Our parents' idea was to prevent us from falling victims to the incessant harassment by the Liberians.

I therefore had to practice my Twi before attempting to speak to the soldiers. After practicing my Twi for a while, I figured out how to initiate a conversation. I gathered courage, approached one of the soldiers as he was passing by, and asked him in Twi, "Are you a Ghanaian?" The soldier was surprised to hear a Ghanaian language from a teenager in the heart of the NPFL territory. He started asking me a lot of questions about my parents in Twi, but I couldn't speak any more Twi beyond my initial question, so I responded in English.

When the soldier heard our story, he could not hold back his tears; it was like a flood gate had been opened. He beckoned a colleague who had also appeared on the scene at that time to go over. He narrated my story to him, and they asked to meet Maa Nuva. I went into the house to call her. When Maa Nuva came out, they exchanged a few pleasantries, then she gave her version of how we went to live with her. They were very glad Maa Nuva helped us. According to her, by some inexplicable means, word had spread around that she was hiding some Ghanaian children in her house. For that reason, she had many visits and interrogations from members of the militias. Her cover-up was that we were her nephew and niece, children of her sister who had been killed in the war. What made her argument believable was that we were light-skinned like she and her daughter were. I remembered that we used to have a lot of people—members of the NPFL—trooping in and out of the house regularly. She always didn't want us to be around when she had the men over. They would always stare at us when they left. I never bordered to find out what they wanted. I also remembered that Maa Nuva used to tell us that whenever someone asked us where we were from, we should tell them she was our aunt and nothing else. That was exactly what I told whoever asked me.

My conversation with the Ghanaian soldiers was very timely because our food had run out and Maa Nuva was wondering how we were going to get food for that week. They asked Maa Nuva if she needed anything, and she asked for some food. They brought her a lot of food and money. It was such a breakthrough for the entire family. That day, almost the entire Ghanaian contingent in the unit went to see us. The younger brother of our father, who was in the army at that time also went to see us. He really resembled our father. He was saddened by the news of the demise of our family and could not hold back his tears. His colleagues had to carry him away because he could not bear the news. He thanked Maa Nuva for helping us and gave her some money before he left. Every soldier who went to see us returned in tears! It was just another tragic end to beautiful lives, stories they had heard repeatedly.

The soldiers reported our case to their superior, who promised to arrange to take us back home to our family in Ghana. Two days later, amidst tears and hugs, we said our final goodbye to Maa Nuva and her daughter and were taken to the ECOMOG headquarters near Freeport. I was very sad to leave Maa Nuva, we had really bonded over that short period. She was such a loving and caring woman. She sacrificed so much to cater to my sister and me. Unfortunately, I lost her contact, and I have not been able to reach out to her. I have also not had the opportunity to visit Liberia ever since.

When we arrived in Central Monrovia, the soldier in charge of us brought us to another Liberian family who took care of us for about three weeks. We ate regularly, were taken to the hospital for health checks, and bought us some new clothes—all in preparation for our trip back to Ghana. The family ensured that we were fit for our journey to Ghana. We had a lot of fun!

In the next chapter, I take you on our journey back to Ghana and how my life took a bizarre turn that set me on a very different trajectory that completely changed my life.

CHAPTER 9

The Journey

At the ECOMOG headquarters located at the Freeport of Monrovia, I was taken to one of the leaders of the Ghanaian troops. He interviewed me to know about my family back in Ghana, but I could only provide very little information. I went to Liberia in 1982, I had never visited Ghana up until that point. Although I remembered the names of some uncles, aunties, and my grandparents, and where they lived in Accra. I did not know the name of the community and how to get there. I thought they could figure it out, but the information I provided did not make it any easy for them to trace my relatives in Ghana.

In my estimation, the most valuable information I provided the man was the name of my grandfather, Seth Korkwei Botchway. Until his retirement in the early 1980s, he served as an assistant commissioner in the Ghanaian Police Service. He was well-known for his crackdown on crime, discipline, and strictness. Fortunately, there was a soldier who bore the same last name as his. He was invited to our meeting, and he happened to be a nephew of our grandfather. According to him, he had not been in touch with my grandfather for some time, but he knew he was still alive and where he lived. I did not know him, and he did not know us either. He added that our grandfather helped his parents finance his education through high school. He agreed to accompany us to Ghana and help us find our family. I guess it was an opportunity for him to visit his family because he had been away for a while.

Around that time, the Ghanaian army had lost two of their men in battle, and they were preparing to transport their bodies to Ghana. The leader decided that it would be a good time to take us back to Ghana. We had to travel by sea to Sierra Leone in a Ghanaian naval boat because the runways at Roberts International Airport in Monrovia had been damaged in the war. From Freeport, we would then be flown to Ghana onboard a military aircraft.

The day of our departure finally arrived, and all was set for our journey back to Ghana. We said our goodbyes to our new family and drove to the shipyard on a military vehicle, where we boarded the naval vessel to set sail to Sierra Leone. I remember that the sun was setting as we left the shores of Freeport, Monrovia, for Freetown, Sierra Leone. As the boat rocked side-to-side before gaining speed, a sense of sadness overwhelmed me. I was leaving without my parents and brother, especially my dear mother, the only friend I had. We went to Liberia as a complete family, but we left Liberia with nothing! What a tragic ending that was for a family that was so promising.

I was also very uncertain about my future. I wondered what life was going to be like without my parents and how my sister and I would be received by our family in Ghana. *Who was going to care for us now that our parents were dead? Since my grandparents had both retired before I left Ghana in 1982, and our mother, on whom the entire family depended had passed, how would her family receive this news? How was our future going to look like? Will I be able to continue my education?* Endless questions just kept running through my mind; I was totally lost in my thoughts. On the other hand, I was happy and relieved that this ugly chapter of my life was closing and I was finally going home to safety.

When the soldiers onboard the naval boat realized that I had been sitting quietly gazing into the horizon for some time, one of them came to us and a few of them gathered around us and engaged me in a conversation. It was helpful because they disrupted my thoughts, and I was able to cheer up for a while. When it was time for our meal, almost all the soldiers onboard brought us some of their food. I guess they simply did the little they could to make us feel okay. Since we had starved for such a long time, we could not resist the food and just kept eating. We ate until we started feeling sick. They kept giving us food even on the plane. At a point, my sister threw up all over me on the plane, probably because she could no longer handle the large quantity of food we were eating or due to motion sickness. Sadly because we were not traveling on a commercial flight, I could not get enough paper towels to clean her up, so I just had to change our clothes.

Arriving in Ghana

We arrived in Ghana on October 27, 1990, at around 11:00 p.m. local time, after about a two-hour flight. It was pretty dark, so I could not see anything as the plane landed. We spent the night in the soldier's house at Burma Camp, the military barracks in Accra.

After breakfast that morning, Sunday, October 28, 1990, the man called me and asked, "Where in Accra did you say your relatives live, and will you find your way home when I take you there?"

His questions caught me off guard. I thought he knew where he was taking us. I had been away from Ghana for eight years and could not remember anything. I was only about seven years old when my mother took me to Liberia. Moreover, a lot had changed over the years that I had been away. I did not even know where I was at that morning, let alone know where to go. I could not recognize Accra; it looked different from the Accra I knew in the 1980s. I was completely lost. There was simply no way I could find my way home. To make matters worse, I had even forgotten all that I told the officer who interviewed me back in Liberia. I was grappling with so many things at that time, and I just didn't have the mind to remember anything. Besides, I could not speak any of the Ghanaian languages. I guess he was just instructed to bring us home, and he did, without gathering all the information he needed.

I simply replied, "I don't remember."

The soldier left my sister and me in the living room and went to discuss the issue with his wife in their room. After a few minutes, he returned to ask me for my full name and went back to speak with his wife.

When I mentioned my name, he said "Great. I will see what I will do."

My tribe—Gã—has a very structured system of naming their children, so much so that once a name was mentioned, anyone familiar with the structure can easily tell the part of Accra you come from: your clan, family, and your position of birth—whether you are the first, second, third born and so on. I guess that helped him to figure out his next line of action.

About five minutes later, he went to tell me that since I don't remember where my family lived in Accra and going by my last name, he knew the part of Accra I come from. He has decided to bring us to the chief of the La traditional area, a suburb of Accra because that is where my name points to as our hometown. He added that the chief knows a lot of people and has structures in place to help us find our relatives. Moreover, he only had a few days in Ghana and had to return to Liberia in a couple of days. The only issue with this idea was that the fact that my name points to that suburb of Accra as my hometown didn't mean that I have lived there or my relatives lived there.

We got ready. He got dressed in his military uniform, as that would give him unhindered access to the chief, and I picked up the little suitcase, and we walked about a few blocks to pick a taxi to the chief's house.

In the next chapter, I will tell you about how a promise of letting the chief help us find our family ended up in an informal adoption and a fifteen-year stay in the chief's house until I married.

Chapter 10

Our New Home

When we arrived at the taxi terminal, there were several taxis there waiting for their turn. We sat in the taxi whose turn it was and we set off. Within twenty minutes, we arrived at the chief's house. The house was built on a huge, walled, and gated yard with many outhouses, unlike anything I was used to in Liberia. There was the main house close to the entrance, and the outhouses were dotted all over the yard. There were so many people in the yard, which was kind of awkward for me because I was not used to having so many people living in a single yard.

The soldier asked to meet the chief, and we were led to a shaded area near one of the outhouses, which was the waiting room, but it was not opened at that time. The young man whom we spoke to returned and opened the door to the waiting room, but the soldier said that we will just sit under the sherd and wait. After a little while, the young man went over to inform us that the chief was ready to see us. The soldier asked me and my sister to wait for him out there, while he went into the main house to meet the chief. After a few minutes, the soldier returned and told me that the chief had agreed to let us stay with him while he sent a message to the various clans and families in his traditional area to find our relatives. According to the soldier, the divisional heads met on Tuesday evenings, and since it was a Saturday, the message will be sent to the various divisions in the suburb through their heads after their traditional council meeting on

Tuesday. The chief went over to where we sat and spoke to us. The soldier then wished us well and left.

I was so disappointed with the arrangement because the soldier didn't fully discuss the plan with me. He just agreed on the plan with the chief. I didn't know anybody in that house, I could not speak the local Gã language at that time, and I didn't know how I was going to communicate with all these strangers. The yard was also too big for my liking, and I just felt that I will have no privacy in that house. I was used to a small family, thus, that situation made me unhappy. Worse of all, within a couple of minutes of the soldier's departure, some children went to where we sat to peek at us. Although I didn't understand what they were talking about, it was obvious from their behavior that they were talking about us because they looked and pointed in our direction. We had all the characteristics of the Liberian refugees, most of whom had sought refuge in Ghana around that time—malnourished, disoriented, scars all over our bodies, and we spoke like the Liberians. I later found out that word spread that some Liberian children had been brought to stay with the chief, which explained why the children were loitering around the place we sat.

Not so long afterward, another young man went over and told me that he had been sent to take me to one of the outhouses on the west side of the main house. My sister was taken by one of the chief's nieces to another outhouse.

When I got to the boys' room, I was disappointed. It was not kept. I was greeted by an unpleasant odor, things lay around haphazardly, the beds were not made, and the room was not even swept. My mother taught me to keep my surroundings very clean, especially my room, so the sight in the room put me off, but I told myself that this was just a temporary arrangement for us for the weekend. I looked forward to Tuesday with eagerness because I was hopeful that my relatives would be found. Within a matter of days, the boys I shared the room with talked me into giving them all the souvenirs I had carried with me from Liberia. It sounds so funny to me as I think about it today because I don't know why they wanted those items in the first place. We were also not placed under the direct care of any specific person, which was kind of strange to me.

A week went by, then another week, then another week, but no one went to claim us as their relatives. I was getting anxious, and no one was telling me anything. The silence from the chief (from here onward, I will refer to him as my dad), and the people in the house was unbearable. I could also not share my anxiety with anyone because I could not speak the Gã language and most of the children in the house were not fluent in English at that time. Besides, I was finding it very hard to adjust to my new lifestyle. I was used to a nuclear family structure, where I could go to my mother or father to discuss my challenges easily with them. I was going through so much emotional stress, but I couldn't speak to anyone about it.

A good example was that I was easily startled by loud noises, especially those that sounded like gunshots: firecrackers. It really freaked me out because it brought me memories of the horror I went through during the war. I had to deal with that trauma all by myself. I had also unknowingly developed the fear of airplanes in flight. Sadly, the house was not so far from the Kotoka International Airport in Accra, which meant that many airplanes landed and took off close to the house and the sound was unnerving for me, especially within the first few days of our arrival. I just had to talk myself out of it. There were many other issues I was grappling with at that time, but I could not open up to anyone. I felt no one showed any concern. I just didn't feel I belonged, and there was no one I could speak to about my emotional distress. I just had to deal with it all by myself and in my way.

I just had to settle quickly into the routine at the house. We woke up early in the morning, swept the yard, took our bath, and when our dad was ready to go to work, he called the boys who ran his errands, gave them money for lunch and off he went. Since I had not started school yet, I just stayed at home, and my dad's older sister, Maa Nkpa, who also lived in the main house but on another side of the house, gave us breakfast and lunch. When my dad returned from work in the evening, he brought a basket of food for dinner, which he gave us, the boys in the house who ran his errands.

One evening in early November 1990, when my dad returned from work, he asked me to accompany him to his house at Mamprobi.

I got ready and we left. Mamprobi is about twelve kilometers away from La. It was a three-bedroom walled house, with a big yard, a lot of trees, and different flowers all around the house. There weren't many people in the house; the kind of environment I was used to. I immediately fell in love with the house; it was a place I could be myself and have some peace. The people who lived in the house were Maa Doris, my dad's wife; Patience, an eleven-year-old girl attending to my dad's wife; Ms. Beatrice (Aunty B), an elderly widow who was the cook and caretaker; and Kwabena, a young artisanal welder, who lived in the outhouse and helped around. On our way back to La, my dad asked me whether I would like to live at Mamprobi or La. It was a very easy decision for me to make because I was already in love with the house and the environment. About a week later, my sister and I packed our things and moved to Mamprobi. I felt much better living there; it was a lot more like a home setting for me than living at La.

Our mother, my dad's wife, was a personnel manager (human resource manager) at the Ghana Cocoa Board, now Ghana Cocoa Authority. She had a structured routine for the weekdays: Her driver went to Mamprobi to pick her up to work in the morning around 7:00 and 7:15 a.m., and she returned with my dad after work, who also worked at the Department of Lotteries, between 5:00 and 6:00 p.m. By then, Aunty B would have prepared dinner. Upon arrival, our mother would go to the kitchen, dish my dad's food, and I will place it in his car. My dad would then stroll around in the yard for a few minutes until he was ready to leave. I, or whoever was less busy at the time, would go open the gate for him and close it when he was gone. Once my dad had left, our mother would have her dinner at the dining hall, initially all by herself, but later, with my sister. We would also then have our food outside the kitchen. When our mother was done, she either went to her room to watch the evening news, which was at 7:00 p.m. on TV, or she would go to her evening meetings at the Nazareth Methodist Church. On Saturday, our mother, Patience, and my sister went to La to spend the weekend.

Our mother seldom interacted with us, except to call me to run errands or give me my chores for the day. Since she did not interact with me very much, it was also very difficult for me to relate to her initially, but that gradually changed. Our mother also became very fond of my sister, who had not yet turned two years old and was simply a joy to have around. She looked forward to chatting with my sister when they went home. I watched with joy how our mother comes alive when she went home in the evenings and how she also talked about my sister's growth and development with her friends and relatives. Not long afterward, my sister became the central focus for both my dad and our mother.

Not so long after we moved to Mamprobi—I think it was about two weeks later—that I turned fifteen. I remember waking up that morning not knowing where my life was headed. I had not yet seen my relatives, and I was not getting any updates from my dad or our mom. I just felt abandoned. I was really hurting inside, but I could not share my feelings with anybody. To make matters worse, I could not speak the Gá language at that time. I had not recovered from my trauma in Liberia, and I wasn't getting the love and attention I needed. Things were getting hard for me each passing day. It was very difficult for me to define my relationship with my new parents.

I remember one evening when my dad and my mother returned from work, he called me into the living room and told me that he had sent messages through all the family heads in the town but no one had shown up to say they are my relatives. He added that he had made a couple of announcements in the local newspaper and a local radio station but to no avail. My dad stated that the year was ending, and he wanted to know what my plans were. "Would you want to continue your education or learn a vocation?" He asked. My mother had always told us that she did not get the chance to go to college so she would want all of us, her children, to be college graduates. The idea of becoming a college graduate was engraved in my mind and heart.

I told my dad that I would like to go back to school. He then asked me what grade I was in Liberia. I told him that I should have completed eighth grade that year, but due to the war, I had not been to school the entire year. He suggested that I should start sixth grade (Junior Secondary School form 1) again because the school systems in Ghana were completely different from that of Liberia and that I needed a record of continuous assessment to be admitted into ninth grade (Senior Secondary School form 1). If I have known any better, I would have suggested that I be taken to high school because that was the grade I should have been in that year. Since I seriously wanted to continue my education, I just agreed to my dad's suggestions. My dad also said he had still not found our relatives, he would like us to bear his last name, Pobee, to make it easy for people to identify us with his family. By some inexplicable circumstance, my dad's family also named my last name, Sowa, but as their middle name. My dad suggested that he would move my last name to be my middle name so that he can give me his last name.

That day, my sister and I became part of the family, but they did not formalize the adoption in a court of law. They did that because he wanted to make it easier for me to take back my name in case I saw my relatives. That gave my dad permission to take care of us without being questioned by anybody. I agreed to my dad's plan because I just wanted to go back to school. I wanted to fulfill the dream my mother put in my heart. I knew that by getting an education, I could honor the memory of my family, especially my mother, who had taught me the essence of education. I knew that going back to sixth grade was a retrogression in my academic progress, but it was, at least, better than me going to learn a trade. This created a huge gap in my education.

When January 1991 school year began, my mother took me to a nearby government school known as Mamprobi Sempe 2, Junior Secondary School (JSS). It was only a ten-minute walk from the house. I feverishly learned to speak and write in the Gã language because I wanted to be able to interact with the people in the community. Aunty B, with whom I used to spend the weekend at Mamprobi, also introduced me to the local Methodist church, Nazareth Methodist Church. I started attending Sunday school, and gradually, I began to help the Sunday School teachers. Not so long afterward, I joined the adult service and started serving there also. I worked extra hard during my first year to learn the Gã language, and I became very fluent in speaking the language.

As I narrated our story, my grandma, did not ask any questions, she just listened. I realized that it was very difficult for her to learn about the harrowing experiences we had lived through. I saw her going on an emotional roller coaster, grinning when the narrative was pleasant and becoming emotional when it was not good.

She was particularly saddened by the loss of our parents and brother in the civil war. She was grateful that we were alive. Grandma wasn't happy that she lost her beloved daughter but grateful that, at least, she had us back. By then, dinner was ready, and she asked that we go have our meal. Grandma also told me that Grandpa left early that morning to attend his regular monthly family meeting in his village, where he served as an elder. That meeting usually lasted the entire day and returned around 7:00 p.m. Grandma added that she was sure that Grandpa would be extremely excited to hear the news that we were alive and living in Ghana.

Not so long after we were done with dinner, my uncle McAdams returned, had some of the meal, and we said goodbye to Grandma and left. It was a very happy day for me because my dream of meeting my family had finally come true.

After this meeting, there was a complete change in my relationship with my new parents, especially my adopted dad. Our relationship became not so good, but it is a story for another time.

CHAPTER 11

My Reflections

In this chapter, I have outlined my thoughts through a series of questions that helped me conclude that a Supreme Being was working through my difficulties to fulfill His purposes. I wanted to know what I had done wrong; why I was suffering so much, and what I had done to deserve all that suffering? Why could I just not have peace of mind and grow up like every ordinary child? I was not a Christian when my ordeals started, but when I became a Christian, they didn't cease; they rather appeared to increase. I asked God so many questions, including where He was when I was going through all those hard times? Why did He allow my mother, father, and brother to be brutally murdered in Liberia for just being what He created them to be—Ghanaians? The war was no fault of theirs, and we were just there trying to make a living. I didn't understand why I had to suffer because of the selfishness of other people?

But guess what? I did not get an immediate answer from God. As I grew in my Christian walk, and I began to search the Scriptures more intensely and carefully, I began to understand of why things were the way they were. It isn't that God didn't care about what I was going through; it was me and other humans who had taken Him out of our affairs. We take Him out of our lives and when things go wrong, we ask Him, "Why?" I began to understand the brokenness of humanity and the world we live in; how evil the human heart had become as a result of sin (see Jeremiah 17:9); how the forces of evil are working against the purposes of God (see Ephesians 6:12; 2 Corinthians 10:3–5).

I believe that God's plan for me was perfect from the beginning; however, there is Satan, the author of all evil, who works tirelessly to thwart the purposes of God in the lives of individuals, especially when he realizes that their continued existence is a threat to his agenda. As John 10:10 (NKJV) says: *"The thief does not come except to steal, and to kill, and to destroy. I have come that they may have life and that they may have it more abundantly."* But God, in His sovereignty, uses both the good and bad situations in our lives to fulfill His divine purposes. Romans 8:28 (NKJV) says that *"And we know that all things work together for good to those who love God, to those who are called according to His purpose."*

Although I wish my life had taken a different turn and things didn't pan out the way they did, I am eternally grateful to God for allowing those horrific experiences to make me a better person today. That reminds me of what the Psalmist says in Psalm 119:71 (NKJV): *"It is good for me that I have been afflicted, That I may learn Your statutes."* It was not a pleasant experience at all, but when I look back over my life—the places I have been, the people I have influenced, the impact I have made, my own family—I can see that Satan wanted to snuff out my light before I could even start and accomplish any of them. God, on the other hand, allowed it because He already knew how things were going to end (see Isaiah 46:9–10), and He already had systems in place to ensure that I will live to fulfill His divine purposes. What the devil meant for evil, God took it and turn it around for good (see Genesis 50:20), and for those reasons, I am eternally grateful to God.

Ravi and Vince wrote in their book, *Why Suffering? Finding Meaning and Comfort When Life Doesn't Make Sense:*

> If God is the author of life, He has an answer to suffering. If something indeed came from nothing, then nothing is the answer to suffering. But if we are the creation of a personal,

moral, infinite, loving God, then He will have the answer for us.[2]

I remember part of Moses' last words and warning to the nation of Israel before his death in Deuteronomy 8:2–5 (NKJV), where he said to them,

> And you shall remember that the Lord your God led you all the way these forty years in the wilderness, to humble you and test you, to know what was in your heart, whether you would keep His commandments or not. So He humbled you, allowed you to hunger, and fed you with manna which you did not know nor did your fathers know, that He might make you know that man shall not live by bread alone, but man lives by every word that proceeds from the mouth of the Lord. Your garments did not wear out on you, nor did your foot swell these forty years. You should know in your heart that as a man chastens his son, so the Lord your God chastens you.

The above verses are very applicable to my life also. God created me to be a carrier of His purpose; however, the circumstances of my birth and life led me far away from that purpose. Satan, for the thief that he is, did his worst to get rid of me. God allowed Satan to take me down to the valley and batter me with fires and floods. However, with every blow from the devil's hammer, God molded me into His desired shape to a point where He could trust me with the reality of His vision. I must admit, it was hard to go through the battering process. Sometimes I wanted to jump off the blacksmith's anvil because the strokes from the hammer were so painful. I like the

---

[2] Zacharias Ravi and Vince Vitale, *Why Suffering? Finding Meaning and Comfort When Life Doesn't Make Sense* (New York: Faith Words, 2014).

way Alfred Lord Tennyson (1809–1892), a popular British poet who lived during much of Queen Victoria's reign puts it:

Life is not as idle ore,
but iron dug from central gloom,
And heated hot with burning fears,
And dipt in baths of hissing tears,
And battered with the shocks of doom,
To shape and use.[3]

I also remember a poem I read some time ago by an unknown author that I identified with. The poem says,

When God wants to drill a man,
And thrill a man,
And skill a man
When God wants to mold a man
To play the noblest part;
When He yearns with all His heart
To create so great and bold a man
That all the world shall be amazed,
Watch His methods, watch His ways!
How He ruthlessly perfects
Whom He royally elects!
How He hammers him and hurts him,
And with mighty blows converts him
Into trial shapes of clay which
Only God understands;
While his tortured heart is crying
And he lifts beseeching hands!
How He bends but never breaks
When his good He undertakes;
How He uses whom He chooses,

---

[3] "Alfred Tennyson Quotes," AZQUOTES, accessed July 6, 2020, https://www. azquotes.com/author/14526-Alfred_Lord_Tennyson.

And which every purpose fuses him;
By every act induces him
To try His splendor out—
God knows what He's about.[4] (Anonymous)

I remember sharing the story of how I was electrocuted with a friend who is an electric engineer and works with the electricity company of Ghana. He didn't believe me because he said there was no way that I could have survived under that high-tension electric cable I was describing. He added that I couldn't have even survived a minute—that is just impossible. Yeah, I also don't believe how I survived that; it *is* impossible! I sometimes doubt that I am the same person who experienced the horror and tragedy narrated in this book. This is because I am a completely changed person. I no longer feel the pain and anguish I used to feel in the past. I remember going to that spot once when I went to visit my grandmother; it was not long after we were found by my uncle. When I reach the exact spot, a sense of gratitude just filled my heart.

When I look back at how I was rescued, the questions that I ask myself are, who was that stranger who helped me that day? I am sure that if that stranger was a minute late I would have died that day. The stranger went onto the scene just in time, when I was losing my breath. But what was he doing out there in the middle of nowhere at 2:00 p.m. on that hot and humid Friday afternoon, when he was supposed to be at work? How did he even know that I was lying there because it was a secluded place? How did he know which house in the neighborhood to take me to? Why did the stranger not give us his name and where he lived? Why did my mother and grandmother not find him when they went to look for him? Could he have been an angel sent to rescue me that day? If he wasn't an angel, then who was he because I cannot think of any possible explanation for his appearance and why he took interest in me.

---

[4] "When God Wants to Drill a Man," Drill A Man, Joni And Friends, last Modified April 20, 2018, www.joniandfriends.org.

What about the night before my mother and brother walked out of the door and never returned? Why did my mother, whom I knew to be a very strong woman, prayed so fervently that night? Did she sense that she was going to die? If she knew, why didn't she tell me to prepare for was what about to unfold? Why was she so restless and unable to sleep that entire night? Why did she keep waking me up? Again, why was there a severe rain and thunderstorm throughout that night into the wee hours of the morning? Was it a clear sign from God that my mother shouldn't go for her sewing machine? Was the sewing machine even worth the risk? As I looked back on that night, I asked myself, why did I not feel a check in my heart or sense that something was not right? Well, I couldn't have realized that something was not right because I did not know God. I was just existing and God did not have a place in my life and family, as such there was no way I could have known. We were not even a normal church-going family, let alone, know how to pray and how God speaks to his children!

My mother was a professing Christian and a Seventh-day Adventist (SDA), but she did not go to church either. Well, her excuse was that there was no SDA church where we lived, which was true. My mother sang a lot of hymns while cooking and doing chores around the house. Two of her favorite songs I remember: "Into my heart, come into my heart Lord Jesus," and "Heavenly Father we appreciate you." My father, on the other hand, spent his Sundays away from the house, refereeing soccer marches. So going to church was not part of our family's activities.

I guess all those events—my mother feeling scared and restless, the heavy downpour, the lightning, and the thunderstorm that occurred that night—were all signs of God's warning of imminent danger. I guess God was telling her not to go for that sewing machine, and that He was going to take care of us. We err simply because we have not learned to recognize the voice of God! I have made it my life-long pursuit to learn to live in constant fellowship with God in order not to jeopardize the life of my wife and children. All my pains, suffering, fears, and uncertainties would have been minimized, if not prevented if my parents knew what I know now. I always want to have that peace of mind and assurance that tells me that God is with me before I take any major decision in life.

My mother waited all morning, and when the rain didn't stop, she went through it to her death! I know my mother was simply driven by her desire to provide for us. She didn't want us to go another day without food. She didn't want to sit idle when she knew she could do something about our situation. She always went to great lengths to provide for us. I am very proud to be the son of a great mother like Ms. Dorothy Ayeh! For those three days that my sister and I lived in that huge school all alone, nothing happened to us; I didn't even have a single nightmare. Although I felt very sad during that period, I always had a sound sleep because God took care of me (see Psalm 4:8). Wouldn't it be right to say that God heard the fervent prayers of my mother?

Come to think of the trauma the school custodian took me through when I showed up at his doorstep that Friday after my mother went missing. Did he know that his refusal to give us food that day and his relentless efforts to get us away from his family was God's way of saving us from dying along with him and his family? Why did the fighting break out that Friday night, when I decided to go and search for my mother the following day? Why did I get so frightened at the shoot-out that I decided to run to the kitchen for safety? Why was there stagnant water in the sink and why was the kitchen full of mosquitoes? Why did I just not leave my little sister behind that morning because she was going to be a drag on my movement that morning?

On our way that morning, where did that Liberian man who walked ahead of us come from when he was nowhere in sight or nowhere on our path until we were approaching the checkpoint and saw him in the distance? That man happened to be the only person we met on our way that morning after we left our neighborhood. Why is it that when we were stopped by the boy soldier, I just didn't ignore that voice that spoke to me and follow through with the lie that I was a Liberian but I spoke the truth? Someone would say it was my conscience or even my mother's spirit that spoke to me that day, but I believe that it was the voice of God that saved me from not going any further. Why did the unit commander not summarily shoot me when he was told that I was a Ghanaian but asked me to give him "six feet," when that was something they did without giving a second thought? What would have happened to me if I had left my sister behind? What would have happened if she did not decide to scream when she saw the gun pointed at us? Who was that strange man and where did he come from? He was not there among the people I met at the scene. Why was he the only sober person among them? Why did he even plead for us when he didn't know us? How was he able to get the attention of that intoxicated young man and have him spare our lives? Did he even know the unit commander?

Could he have been the same man who went to my rescue some eight years earlier, when I lay dying under the live electric wire? He could have been a guiding angel sent to our rescue because I have no logical explanation for why he went to our aid. I had never seen him before that day nor ever seen him afterward. His intervention was so critical and timely that if he was a minute late, the commander would have shot me. If this was not divine intervention, then I don't know what to call it! You may not believe in the existence and activities of angels, but I believe that the stranger was an angel God sent to rescue me and my sister.

Why did the unit commander ask where I was going that morning? Why did he even care if I was killed when I go beyond his area of operation? Was he not the same person who said he shot my mother and brother three days earlier? Why did he even ask me whether I had eaten that day? Why did he even ask whether I knew how to cook or not? Why did the unit commander ask the boy soldier to go to the storage and get me some food? From the little I knew about those young soldiers at that time, they were heartless and didn't care whether you lived or died when you crossed their paths. The fact that he had the mind to think about our well-being in his intoxicated state falls short of nothing but a miracle.

On our way back, why did it start to rain when I stepped out of the bushes onto the soccer field? Why did Maa Nuva and her daughter decide to be on their front porch at that particular time? Why did I decide to greet them when it was risky? If I had left my sister behind, would Maa Nuva have asked us where we were going in the rain? If my sister's eyes were not swollen as a result of us sleeping in the kitchen, would Maa Nuva have taken notice of us? Why did Maa Nuva, who did not know us, have compassion for us?

What about the circumstances surrounding how my family found me? I had been living in that house at Mamprobi for over a year and my uncle had been going to our neighborhood's barbering saloon for a long time, yet our paths never crossed until that day. Can we say it was a coincidence that I met my uncle that day? Why did I even decide to tie the feet of the roosters the way I did that day? Why did I not tie them the usual way I did all the time? How did the roosters vanish out of my sight? Why was I not able to find them for more than fifteen minutes? How did those roosters get outside the yard when there was no way they could have gotten out? Why was my uncle leaving the saloon just when I got to the scene?

My questions can go on without end, but all the answers can be summarized in this one statement: "God loves me so much that He didn't allow my troubles to kill me, but He used them as instruments to break all the dross in my life, mold me into a vessel of honor, and fill me with His power and glory to accomplish His purposes on earth. When I look back over the events of my life, I am convinced that the devil has been working to destroy me; he wanted me dead even before I took my first breath. A common statement people who hear my story always make is that 'the hand of God is on you and you will not die until that purpose is accomplished." The Psalmist says that "*I shall not die, but live, and declare the works of the LORD*" (Psalm 118: 17), and I believe it with all my heart!

As I mentioned earlier, my challenges did not go away when I became a Christian, but they have made me a better person. I am now able to empathize with people and understand life's challenges from their point of view because I have been there. I never had access to the services of a psychologist to help me deal with my grief, and nor did I have anyone to run to for help, but I had a faithful God who stood by me and helped me through those difficult moments. Initially, I didn't have any other outlet for my pain and grief, except to weep, but as I grew in Christ, I began to channel my grief through reading the bible, praying, and listening to gospel music, initially from gospel artists from Integrity Music, especially, Don Moen, then Ron Kenoly and others. At a point, I started composing and arranging my music, learning to play different musical instruments, and now, writing books. I also became a lay preacher in the Methodist Church, a youth leader, a music minister, a worship leader, a music director, a bible class leader, a church elder (in three different churches I have been a member of over the years), a youth mentor, and a counselor.

Today, whenever I face any challenge, I would simply look back to the events in Liberia, as well as the challenges I had in Ghana, and draw strength from them. I would remind myself of God's goodness and how that had sustained me. I would say things like, "If God did not allow me to perish in Liberia, where no one was certain of living to see another day, He will bring me out of this also." So long as I am praying and staying away from sin and transgression, God has my back; and whatever trial I am facing at this moment will also pass because *I am destined to survive*! I believe Scripture with all my heart because I have seen it play out in my life. I know that God will not allow any of my pain to be wasted, no way! My pain will never be in vain if I allow Him to use my story to His glory. Although I wished my life had played out a little differently, I am thankful God chose to do it this way—through pain and suffering!

At the time of writing this book, it had been thirty long years since the tragic events that occurred in Liberia, but the scenes of those days are still vivid in my mind as though they occurred just yesterday. When I look at my life today—how far I have come over these years, my struggles, fears, tears, challenges, hopes, and successes—it is obvious that the prayers our mother offered that night, Tuesday, August 28, 1990, were answered. I would not say I have arrived or my life is without challenges, but only one thing has been certain—God's love has protected and provided for my sister and me! We have been shown so much mercy in life! *I am indeed destined to survive!*

BIBLIOGRAPHY

Wikipedia. "First Liberian Civil War." Accessed April 13, 2020. https://en.wikipedia.org/wiki/First_Liberian_Civil_War.

Zacharias, Ravi, and Vince Vitale. *Why Suffering? Finding Meaning and Comfort When Life Doesn't Make.* New York: Faith Words, 2014.

JoniAndFriends. "When God Wants to Drill a Man." Drill A Man. Last Modified April 20, 2018. www.joniandfriends.org.

About the Author

Leslie Pobee is a geographical information systems (GIS) analyst/ data scientist by profession. He is also a music minister with a strong passion for promoting quality music and raising worship leaders. He has rich experience with an outstanding record of ministry in Africa, Europe, and the USA. Leslie is a recording artist and has written over fifty songs and currently working on several new singles. He is married with three children.